Where Are They Now?

Andy Pringle
& Neil Fissler

Dedicated to
Peter Fissler
(31st January 1940 to 1st October 2008)
"The world's greatest Manchester United fan."

First published in 2010 by
Media House Books
PO Box 466, Eastleigh
Hampshire SO50 0AA
02380 740400
info@mediahousebooks.co.uk

ISBN 978 0 9554937 4 4

Printed and bound in Great Britain by Hobbs the Printers Ltd, Southampton

Introduction

You may not be surprised to learn that the idea of 'Where Are They Now?' was first discussed in a pub! A pre-match conversation one wet Saturday was triggered by the sight of a couple of former players who hadn't been seen for a few years. We wondered what they had been doing since retiring from the game and the idea for a book was born.

It was a great excuse (and fairly surreal) to meet famous former players and to wallow in nostalgia with the characters who had made growing up as a football fan so exciting.

The first edition was effectively self-published and very quickly became an 'underground' hit. 1,000 copies were printed and sold out almost immediately. Remarkably, it can still be found advertised on Amazon.

Labelled the 'Bog-readers Bible' and the 'Anorak's Almanac', it appeared to capture the imagination and was regularly listed by the Sunday Times as the best selling sports book of the week.

The second edition quickly followed and this also proved to be a major success, again topping the best selling sports book charts.

That was back in 1996, but the thrill of the hunt remained as strong as ever and has prompted us to track down some of the most famous names to have ever worn the famous red shirt.

A project like this couldn't have been possible without the help of many people, most notably Leigh Edwards, who has been a constant source of information and entertainment especially in times of nous failure. A big thank you also goes out to the host of kind people who supplied the varied selection of photos which have helped make this book what it is.

We hope you enjoy the read.

Neil Fissler (London), Andy Pringle (Romsey)

ABBOTT, Peter

Appearances: 0 Goals: 0 (1970-1974)
Career: *Manchester United, Swansea City, Crewe Alexandra, Southend United (1970-1980).* Joined United as an apprentice in July 1970 after turning down offers from seven other clubs. Became Wilf McGuinness's first professional signing after he succeeded Sir Matt Busby, having been a regular in the Central League team from the age of sixteen. Despite being a professional for more than four years at United, he failed to make a first team appearance. Moved to Swansea, initially on loan in February 1974, when he was spotted by Harry Gregg in a practice match. He signed permanently a month later. He now lives in Rudyard and has a successful swim school in Stoke-on-Trent, is also the head coach of Biddulph Amateur Swimming Club.

ALBISTON, Arthur

Appearances: 485 Goals: 7 (1974-1988)
Career: *Manchester United, West Bromwich Albion, Chesterfield, Chester City (1974-1993).* What Arthur lacked in height he certainly made up for in other areas, being incredibly quick and strong in the tackle. In the thirteen years that his name appeared on United's books, he managed to clock up over 350 appearances and to this day, still ranks among the club's longest serving players. He won 15 caps for Scotland and appeared in three FA Cup victories before moving to West Bromwich Albion on a free transfer in 1988. After further stops at Dundee, Chesterfield and Chester, the former Scottish international became manager of Drolysden in the North West Counties League. Worked as a junior coach at United for four years and has also worked as a summariser for Manchester Independent radio station. Now works for MUTV as a match summariser on reserve and youth team games.

Arthur Albiston
Photo: United Nights

ALLEN, Reginald

Appearances: 75 Goals: 0 (1950-1953)
Career: *Queens Park Rangers, Manchester United (1938-1953).* All round sportsman and former army commando, was POW in North Africa after being captured in a World War Two raid. United paid £11,000 and broke the transfer record for a keeper to procure his services from Queens Park Rangers in 1950. Helped win the League Championship in 1951-1952 before retiring in 1953. He settled in Ealing and did various jobs. He died in April 1976, a month before his 56th birthday, after suffering from ill health.

ANDERSON, John

Appearances: 33 Goals: 1 (1938-1949)
Career: *Manchester United, Nottingham Forest, Peterborough United (1938-1954).* Became the first player post-World War Two in 1948 to win a FA Cup winner's medal in his debut season, he scored in the 4-2 victory over Blackpool. The son of a former rugby league player, he made his debut in December 1947 as a late replacement for Johnny Carey, but he couldn't hold down a regular place in United's half back line. Later worked as a coach and briefly caretaker manager at his last club, Peterborough. He died in Manchester in August 2006, aged 84.

ANDERSON, Trevor

Appearances: 19 Goals: 2 (1972-1974)
Career: *Manchester United, Swindon Town, Peterborough United (1972-1978).* Arrived for £20,000 to replace another Belfast native George Best. Frank O'Farrell, who signed him was sacked within a matter of weeks but he repaid new boss Tommy Docherty by scoring a vital goal against Leeds. Although this helped avoid relegation he was later discarded by The Doc. Worked as a clerk in Belfast City Hospital, which he combined with a successful career in football management with Linfield, Newry Town, Ards and Dundalk.

ANDERSON, Viv

Appearances: 68 Goals: 3 (1987-1991)
Career: *Nottingham Forest, Arsenal, Manchester United, Sheffield Wednesday, Barnsley (1974-1993).* The first black footballer to play for England, he was Sir Alex Ferguson's first ever signing for the club for a tribunal set fee of £250,000. He held down a regular place in the first team for the vast majority of his four seasons at Old Trafford but missed out on the 1990 FA Cup Final when Paul Ince was preferred at right back. Was released on a free transfer and had a spell as player/manager at Barnsley before joining his old United pal, Bryan Robson at Middlesbrough FC, as his assistant for seven seasons. He is now a highly successful businessman with several consulting and ambassadorial roles.

ANDERSON, Willie

Appearances: 12 Goals: 0 (1963-1967)
Career: *Manchester United, Aston Villa, Cardiff City (1963-1976).* An FA Youth Cup winner in 1963-1964 after joining United straight from school, made his league debut as a 16 year old on the opposite wing to another rookie, George Best. He found that his chances were limited even though he played in a FA Cup and European Cup semi-finals and was sold to Aston Villa in January 1967 for £20,000. Moved to Oregon, USA to work as an executive with a local radio station. He is also coaching BSC Portland. Has coached for eight years in the Portland area, formally with FC Portland.

Viv Anderson Photo: *Global Imagination*

APPLETON, Michael

Appearances: 2 Goals: 0 (1994-1997)
Career: *Manchester United, Lincoln City, Grimsby Town, Preston North End, West Bromwich Albion (1994-2003).*
A lifelong United fan, he progressed through the ranks and made his debut in a League Cup tie with Swindon Town. His second and final game, was a defeat at Leicester City. He joined Preston North End for a then club record £500,000 at the end of the 1996-1997 season. Michael retired from football in 2003 from a serious knee injury. He returned to West Bromwich Albion to become the club's Academy Manager, before moving on to Reserve Team Manager and is currently First Team Coach.

ASTBURY, Tommy

Career: *Manchester United. War Time guest.* Played for United in the North Final of the Football League War Cup defeat to Bolton Wanderers. Astbury worked for a building supplies firm and was an ex-captain and lifelong vice-president of Hawarden Golf Club. He died in 1993, aged 73, in Flintshire.

ASTON (Snr), John

Appearances: 282 Goals: 30 (1946-1955) Career: *Manchester United (1946-1955).* A one club man who joined United, initially as an amateur player in 1937. He finally left the club in 1972 by which time he had become the club's Chief Scout.

Father of John Jnr, the former inside forward won 17 England caps from his adopted role in defence. He helped lift the FA Cup in 1948 and won himself a League Championship medal in 1952. Forced to retire from playing due to ill health in 1955, John continued to work behind the scenes. From 1956 until his final departure in 1972 he held a number of posts in the Old Trafford back room set up, including junior coach and then chief scout to Wilf McGuiness. After leaving the club he briefly scouted for Luton Town and Birmingham City before going to work with his son in the family pet food business. Died in July 200, aged 81.

John Aston with David Sadler
Photo: Sporting Memorabilia

ASTON (Jnr), John

Appearances: 187 Goals: 27 (1964-1972) Career: Manchester United, Luton Town, Mansfield Town, Blackburn Rovers (1964-1981). A flying winger who provided crosses for many of the greats. Had the game of his life in the 1968 European Cup Final victory over Benfica at Wembley, he won a League Championship winner's medal in 1966-1967. A broken leg at the start of 1968-1969 season against Manchester City at Maine Road signalled the beginning of the end of his career at the club but it wasn't until 1972 that he was sold to Luton Town for £30,000. Later played for Mansfield Town and Blackburn Rovers. His father, John Ashton (Snr), also played for United. Retired from football in 1981. Set up his own pet shop, Pet World, in Stalybridge.

BAARTZ, Ray

Appearances: 0 Goals: 0 (1963-1966)
Career: *Manchester United (1963-1966)*. Moved to Old Trafford along with Newcastle's Adamstown-Rosebuds' teammate Doug Johns as a 17 year old initially on a six-month scholarship deal. He stayed on after Johns returned home, impressed Sir Matt Busby enough to be offered a two year contract. He was a regular for United's reserves but because he didn't qualify for a work permit, he was unable to play for United's first team. It came as a surprise to Busby in 1966 when he announced he was homesick and wanted to go home to Australia. Sydney Hokoah paid an Australian record £5,600 to secure his signature. The Australian football legend returned to his native Newcastle where he ran his own successful sports store business until retiring.

Photo: jacashgone

BAILEY, Gary

Appearances: 373 Goals: 0 (1978-1987)
Career: *Manchester United (1978-1987)*. Paid his own air fare from South Africa to Manchester for a trial but quickly established himself as a top quality goalkeeper following the retirement of Alex Stepney. Appeared in a Wembley Cup Final at the end of his first season which ended in a defeat to Arsenal, he went onto pick up two winner's medals in 1983 and 1985. He earned the nickname of Dracula because of his fear of crosses. A serious knee injury picked up on international duty ended his career when he was at his peak, and his contract was cancelled in September 1987. Born in Ipswich, son of Roy (Crystal Palace and Ipswich), Gary, an England International goalkeeper, has spent much of his life in Johannesburg where he settled and became an anchorman on South African television channel Supersport. After starting his media career in radio, he was an ambassador for South Africa's bid to host the 2010 World Cup.

BAIRD, Henry

Appearances: 53 Goals: 18 (1936-1938)
Career: *Manchester United, Huddersfield Town, Ipswich Town (1936-1951)*. Northern Ireland international wing half, joined United for £3,500 in January 1937 but he took his time settling into a struggling team and they were relegated. The following season, he found his feet scoring 15 times in the League and FA Cup, helping them to secure promotion as runners up to Aston Villa but was sold to Huddersfield just before World War Two. He became a team coach with Ipswich Town before returning to Belfast, where he died in 1973, aged 60.

BAKER, Dessie

Appearances: 0 Goals: 0 (1994-1996)
Career: *Manchester United (1994-1996)*. Spent two years in the United youth team and was a FA Youth team winner before he was released without being offered a professional contract, and he returned to Ireland to sign for Shelbourne. He has been playing for Shamrock Rovers since 2008.

BALDWIN, Tommy

Appearances: 2 Goals: 0 (1974-1975)
Career: *Arsenal, Chelsea, Millwall, Manchester United, Brentford (1964-1977). Having made a name for himself at Chelsea,* Baldwin joined United on loan from Millwall to cover for Stuart Pearson, made his league debut against Sunderland at Roker Park in January 1975 but soon returned to the capital. He now lives in Fulham, West London and has worked in property development and the media.

BALL, John

Appearances: 23 Goals: 0 (1947-1949)
Career: *Manchester United, Bolton Wanderers (1948-1958).* Found his chances at Old Trafford very limited because he had to understudy one of the greatest full backs in the club's history, Johnny Carey. Because of the lack of first team chances, he made the short move to Bolton Wanderers in exchange for Harry McShane. Managed Wigan Athletic for three seasons before leaving the game and he became a painter and decorator before emigrating to Australia.

BALL, John Thomas

Appearances: 50 Goals: 18 (1929-1930 & 1933-1934)
Career: *Southport, Manchester United, Sheffield Wednesday, Manchester United, Huddersfield Town, Luton Town (1929-1936).* Legend has it that when United's chief scout, Louis Rocca, wanted to beat off the competition from several other clubs to sign the highly rated Ball, he picked him up from his home one Sunday in a taxi and drove around all day until they had shaken off the competition. His first spell at Old Trafford only lasted a few months before he was sold to Sheffield Wednesday when the club needed cash, only to return two and a half years later in part exchange for Neil Dewar.

He created history in September and October 1934 when he appeared in all three divisions in a six week spell. He ended his career at Luton Town where he missed one game against Bristol Rovers through injury and his stand-in, Joe Payne, scored ten goals! He spent 20 years working for Vauxhall Motors before joining a wholesale manufacturing chemist. He was a masseur in his spare time and in retirement, helped out behind the bar of his son's pub. He died in February 1976, aged 69.

BAMFORD, Thomas

Appearances: 109 Goals: 57 (1934-1938) Career: *Wrexham, Manchester United, Swansea Town (1929-1946).* A forward who scored seven goals in his first six games for the club to set up the march to the 1935-1936 Second Division Championship, but then the goals dried up in the First Division as United's fortunes slumped. 14 goals in 23 games in the 1937-1938 season aided another successful promotion campaign. He returned to Wrexham after retiring and worked in a local steelworks until his death in December 1967 aged 62.

BANNISTER, Jimmy

Appearances: 61 Goals: 8 (1906-1910)
Career: *Manchester City, Manchester United, Preston North End, Port Vale (1902-1912).* Moved across Manchester after he was made available for transfer after being banned, following an illegal payments scandal. Won the League title during his first season at United, only missing two games. Bannister played less regularly the next season, before losing his inside right berth altogether. He took a move closer to home by signing for Preston North End in October 1909. He was the landlord of the Ship Inn in his native Leyland for a number of years.

BARBER, Jack

Appearances: 4 Goals: 2 (1922-1924)
Career: *Manchester United, Southport, Halifax Town, Rochdale, Stockport Count (1922-1933).* He spent two years mainly in the reserves partly due to a run of bad luck with injuries and was allowed to join Southport. He worked as a joiner in Bacup where he was also secretary of the local football team, Bacup Borough. He later worked as a mill engineer in Manchester. He died in March 1961, aged 60.

BARDSLEY, Phil

Appearances: 18 Goals: 0 (2003-2008)
Career: *Manchester United, Burnley, Aston Villa, Sheffield United, Sunderland (2003-2010).* Went to the same school as former United team mate Mark Howard, he grew up near the Cliff. He signed apprentice forms having been at the club since the age of eight. After a handful of first team appearances and following a succession of loan spells, he signed for Sunderland in January 2008.

BARNES, Michael

Appearances: 1 Goals: 0 (2006-2008)
Career: *Manchester United, Chesterfield, Shrewsbury Town (2006-2008).* Signed after a successful trial, after being spotted playing in the FA Youth Cup for Lancaster City. He progressed through the youth team and reserves into the first team, making his only appearance in a League Cup tie

Photo: O. Taillon

against Crewe Alexandra. He was sent out on loan but when United ditched one of their reserve teams, he was handed a free transfer in June 2008. He now plays for AFC Halifax after spells at Northwich Victoria and Southport.

BARNES, Peter

Appearances: 25 Goals: 4 (1985-1987)
Career: *Manchester City, West Bromwich Albion, Leeds United, Coventry City, Manchester United, Manchester City, Bolton Wanderers, Port Vale, Hull City, Bolton Wanderers, Sunderland (1974-1988).* Barnes had a brief spell at Old Trafford on loan in May 1984 before linking up with his former WBA boss, Ron Atkinson, 13 months later in a £50,000 deal. He was outstanding to start off with as they chalked up ten successive victories but then his form faded along with that of the rest of the team, as soon as Alex Ferguson took over he was quickly shipped out of the door in a £30,000 return to Maine Road. He has worked in radio, TV, coaching and scouting. Was the director of Kick Off Soccer Centre, has been involved with a company that sells artificial pitches, and has also worked at City in their hospitality suites.

BARTHEZ, Fabien

Appearances: 139 Goals: 0 (2000-2004)
Career: *Manchester United (2000-2004).* Signed from Monaco for £7.8 million as the long term replacement for Peter Schmeichel and he soon became a crowd favourite at Old Trafford because of his eccentric behaviour. He won Premier League winner's medals in 2000-2001 and 2003-2003. One mistake too many against Real Madrid in the Champions League brought an end to his time at the club. Tim Howard was bought into replace him and he joined Marseille on loan the following New Year. He has been seen on the beach soccer and poker circuits.

Photo: ypauleau

Photo: United States Marine Corps

BARSON, Frank

Appearances: 152 Goals: 4 (1922-1928)
Career: *Barnsley, Aston Villa, Manchester United, Watford, Hartlepool United (1911-1930).* One of the most controversial figures of his day, is said to have been sent off 12 times during his career. He picked up many lengthy suspensions including one following the 1926 FA Cup Final against Manchester City, when he fouled Sam Cowan who was knocked out. He was popular throughout his six years at Old Trafford and helped the club win promotion in 1925. Was given a free transfer at the age of 37, three years later. A blacksmith by trade, he was promised a pub if he captained United to promotion and when he did, he took over a hotel in Ardwick Green but walked out after 15 minutes after getting fed up of admirers. He joined the Aston Villa coaching staff in 1935 before moving to Swansea Town 12 years later. He stayed in South Wales until 1954 when he returned to Birmingham working for Lye Town until his retirement. He died in September 1968.

BEARDSLEY, Peter

Appearances: 1 Goals: 0 (1982-1983)
Career: *Carlisle United, Manchester United, Newcastle United, Liverpool, Everton, Bolton Wanderers, Man City, Fulham, Hartlepool United (1979-1999).*
Signed by Ron Atkinson for £250,000 after a trial, on the recommendation of Jimmy Murphy who thought the raw striker would go on to become a leading star. But he only got one chance in the first team squad in a League Cup against Bournemouth, and with the likes of Mark Hughes and Norman Whiteside coming through, he was allowed to return to the Vancouver Whitecaps. After retiring, he joined the coaching staff at Newcastle United. He then worked in a media role before being appointed an academy coach in 2009 and promoted to run the reserves in 2010.

BEARDSMORE, Russell

Appearances: 73 Goals: 4 (1988-1993)
Career: *Manchester United, Blackburn Rovers, AFC Bournemouth (1988-1998).*
One of the original Fergie's Fledglings, he announced his arrival in the first team in style scoring one and setting up two in only his second game. He became a first team regular for the rest of the 1988-1989 season following the departure of Gordon Strachan, but a loss of form and injuries saw him return to the reserves. Following the arrival of Paul Ince and Neil Webb, his chances became fewer and in the end he was granted a free transfer. After a serious back injury ended his career, he returned to the north west to work as assistant community officer at Bolton before joining Bournemouth's coaching staff.

BECKHAM, David

Appearances: 394 Goals: 85 (1992-2003) Career: *Manchester United, Preston (1992-2003).* Now the most recognisable football icon on the planet. He was lured to Old Trafford under the noses of several London clubs including Spurs, where he played for four years as a junior. He made his United debut in a league Cup tie with Brighton in 1992, before having a spell on loan at Preston. He was part of United's 1992 and 1994 FA Youth Cup Final successes and became a household name after scoring from the halfway line in a game against Wimbledon at Selhurst Park. He made the United number seven shirt his own to rank alongside Eric Cantona, George Best, Bryan Robson and Cristiano Ronaldo. He was part of United's historic treble winning team in 1999 but soon afterwards, his relationship with Sir Alex deteriorated. In August 2003, he was sold to Real Madrid for £25 million. Now living in L.A., with his wife Posh Spice Victoria Beckham and his family, he plays for the LA Galaxy and has had two spells playing for AC Milan in the MLS closed season.

BEHAN, Billy

Appearances: 1 Goals: 0 (1933-1934)
Career: *Manchester United (1933-1934)*. The first Irish keeper in United's history to play a league game when he appeared against Bury at Old Trafford in March 1934, he conceded a goal in the first minute. It turned out to be his only game for the club after the signing of former England keeper, Jack Hacking, and he returned to Shelbourne. He lived in Dublin and worked as United's scout in the Republic of Ireland discovering Johnny Carey, Billy Whelan, Johnny Giles, Kevin Moran, Gerry Daly and Paul McGrath among others. He retired in 1987, four years before his death in November 1991, aged 80.

BELL, Alec

(1903-1913)
Career: *Manchester United, Blackburn Rovers (1903-1915)*. Born in South Africa to Scottish parents, joined United from Scottish football for £750 as a centre forward, but the club needed half backs and converted him into a left half. He was a regular in the team for a decade and formed part of the famous half back line of Bell, Charles Roberts and Dick Duckworth. Won two Championships and an FA Cup before leaving for Blackburn Rovers in a £1,000 deal, winning another title in his first season. He became a trainer at Coventry City before moving back to Manchester to work in a similar capacity at City until his death in Chorlton-Cum-Hardy, in November 1934, aged 52.

BELLION, David

Appearances: 40 Goals: 8 (2003-2005)
Career: *Sunderland, Manchester United, West Ham United (2001-2006)*. He struggled to make an impression at the club after his controversial move from Sunderland. He scored on his debut against Celtic on the United's pre-season tour of the USA in 2003-2004.

The following season was spent largely in the reserves while 2005-2006 was spent on loan at West Ham and then Nice, who he joined permanently later in June 2006. He left Nice for Bordeaux in 2007 and has spent the last three seasons playing there.

BENNION, Ray

Appearances: 301 Goals: 3 (1921-1932)
Career: *Manchester United, Burnley (1921-1934)*. A Welsh international half back, was playing in the Cheshire County League when he wrote to United to request a trial. He went straight into the reserves and helped them win the Central League. He was signed to understudy Clarence Hilditch and his league debut ended in a 5-0 defeat at the hands of Everton in August 1921. He became popular with the crowd and was a regular in the first team for 11 seasons but he rejected United's terms for the 1932-1933 season and joined Burnley on a free transfer. Retiring in 1934, he joined the Turf Moor coaching staff and held the post of trainer until being forced to retire through ill health in February 1964, four years after the club won the League Championship. He remained in the town until his death in March 1968, aged 72.

BENT, Geoff

Appearances: 12 Goals: 0 (1954-1956)
Career: *Manchester United (1954-1956)*. The understudy to United skipper Roger Byrne so therefore found his chances limited, he was cool, calm and composed whenever he was called upon, and was never on the losing team when he played. Tragically killed in the Munich air disaster and is buried in St John's Churchyard in Pendlebury. He was included in the United party travelling to Belgrade, after Byrne sustained a minor knock in the Babes' last League game together against Arsenal.

Photo: Andy Welsh

BEST, George

Appearances: 361 Goals: 137
Career: *Manchester United, Stockport County, Fulham, Bournemouth (1963-1982).* If judged on pure ability alone, George Best was unquestionably one of the most naturally gifted footballers of all time. However, it is sad to reflect that such skill was often overshadowed by his off the field activities. Even though it all went wrong later, United fans did have ten years of enjoying the Belfast boy's magical skills. During that time, the European Cup was lifted as were two League titles. George himself was awarded the Player of the Year trophy, was voted European Footballer of the Year and made 37 appearances for Northern Ireland. When an unsettled social life started to affect his playing, he went on his travels, making appearances for a succession of clubs. Although unable to replicate the artistry achieved while at his peak, he never lost the ability to pull a crowd and entertain

them like no-one else before or since. One of the greatest ever individual players of all time. Made his debut for Manchester United at the age of 17 and played his first game for Ireland before his 18th birthday. In 1968, he became both British and European Footballer of the Year. After brief spells With Fulham and Bournemouth, played in America League before ending his competitive playing days, many believe far too early. Latterly made his living though public and media appearances, both at home and abroad. Also toured the country with Rodney Marsh in a popular stage double act. Died on 25th November 2005 in the Cromwell Hospital, London. (Won two League championship medals and a European Cup winner's medal.)

BERG, Henning

Appearances: 103 Goals: 3 (1997-2000)
Career: *Blackburn R, Manchester U, Blackburn R (1993-2003).* A member of an elite band of players to win the Premier League title with two different clubs.

George Best's grave.
Photo: Las Orejas de Ringo

United paid £5 million for him which was a British record fee for a defender at the time. He was part of the famous treble winning squad in 1999 even though he missed the two Finals through injury. He was also part of the squad which retained their domestic crown 12 months later, but he returned to Blackburn the following season. Berg was appointed manager of Lynn Oslo in his native Norway in 2005. In 2008, he left to re-join former club Lillestrom as manager on a five-year contract.

BERRY, John

Appearances: 247 Goals: 37 (1951-1958) Career: Birmingham City, Manchester United (1944-1958). Although relatively short at 5ft 5in, John was a true competitor, fast on the wing and never afraid to take on a defender no matter how tough their reputation. A former Army player from Aldershot, he started his time as a professional by signing for Birmingham City after the war. A target that Matt Busby had long had his eye on, his services were finally secured in 1951 by parting with a transfer fee of £25,000. Winner of four England caps and three championship medals, the diminutive livewire never recovered sufficiently from injuries sustained at Munich to recommence his already successful career. He opened a sports shop with his brother Peter, who played for Crystal Palace and Ipswich Town, in Farnborough, Hampshire. He died in September 1994, aged just 68. He was the first of the surviving players from the Munich air crash to die.

BETTS, Denis

Appearances: 0 Goals: 0
Career: A youth team player who opted not to make his career football, instead played rugby league where he won six championships, seven Challenge Cups, three Premierships, four John Player/Regal Trophies and two

Lancashire Cups. He also received the Lance Todd Trophy (1991) and the coveted Man of Steel award in 1995 while playing for Wigan. He joined the Wigan coaching staff before switching codes to work for Gloucester. He left Kingsholm in June 2010.

BIELBY, Paul

Appearances: 4 Goals: 0 (1973-1974) Career: Manchester United, Hartlepool United, Huddersfield Town (1973-1979). Played in the same England youth teams as Peter Barnes, Bryan Robson, Ray Wilkins and Glenn Hoddle. Made his league debut in the explosive Manchester derby in March 1974 which saw two players sent off, four booked and Clive Thomas take both teams off the pitch at one stage. He left Old Trafford to return to his native North East after two seasons. Lives in his native Harrowgate, Darlington. Worked his way up from sales rep to the board of directors of Hazlewood Foods, he is now a players' agent, also works as a motivational speaker and formed the Masterskills Football Academy in his home town.

BIRCH, Brian

Appearances: 15 Goals: 5 (1949-1952) Career: *Manchester United, Wolves, Lincoln City, Barrow, Exeter City, Oldham Athletic, Rochdale (1949-1962).* An England youth international, made his United debut against WBA in August 1949 as a 17 year old. He enjoyed his best season in 1950-51 when he scored four goals in eight first team games. But faced with stiff competition for places despite averaging a goal in every three games, he was sold to Wolves for a five figure fee. He embarked on a coaching career by becoming juniors coach at Blackburn Rovers in 1967, he went on to manage Galatasaray, twice taking them to much success. He later had spells in Sweden and Egypt before settling in South Africa.

BIRTLES, Garry

*Appearances: 64 Goals: 12 (1980-1982)
Career: Nottingham Forest, Manchester
United, Nottingham Forest, Notts
County, Grimsby Town (1976-1993).*
Dave Sexton paid Nottingham Forest
£1.25m for him in 1980 but he failed to
live up to his billing. He failed to settle
with partners Joe Jordan and then Frank
Stapleton, and despite a couple of false
starts when it looked like he might
become the player his talent deserved,
he returned to the City Ground after two
disappointing years for a cut price
£250,000 after only managing to score
12 goals. Lives in Nottingham and had a
fish business in Grimsby. Is now a co-
commentator on Sky Sports, has
previously worked on radio
commentaries for Radio Nottingham.
He also writes a weekly column in the
Nottingham Evening Post.

BLACKMORE, Clayton

*Appearances: 245 Goals: 26 (1982-
1994) Career: Manchester United,
Middlesbrough, Bristol City, Barnsley,
Notts County (1982-2000).* Versatile
Welshman from Neath who spent ten
years as a professional following his
apprenticeship. During this time, he
was used primarily as a squad player
however this did not prevent him
notching up a total of over 200 League
and Cup appearances, and was capped
by Wales on 39 occasions. Finally
allowed to leave in 1994 when he linked
up with former team mate Bryan
Robson at Middlesbrough. Blackmore
has previously been player manager of
Welsh clubs Bangor City and
Porthmadog. He briefly returned as a
player for Neath Athletic. He is now
back at United coaching the Under-15s
and Under-16s after being involved in
hospitality and television work at the
club. He is also an after dinner speaker.

Clayton Blackmore (second from right) with Alex Stepney and David May.
Photo: United Nights

BLANC, Laurent

Appearances: 75 Goals: 4 (2001-2003)
Career: *Manchester United (2001-2003).*
It took several attempts from Sir Alex
Ferguson to land his man but he finally
managed it in 2001, when he needed a
replacement for Jaap Stam. He took his
time to settle but eventually helped the
club to the 2002-2003 Premier League
crown in his last season before retirement.
He became coach of Bordeaux in 2007,
staying until the end of the 2009-2010
season when he left to take over as
coach of the French national team.

BLANCHFLOWER, Jackie

*Appearances: 117 Goals: 27 (1951-
1958)* Career: *Manchester United (1951-
1958).* Adaptable player who was
equally at home in defence or attack,
and even pulled on the goalie's jersey
during the 1957 FA Cup final when Ray
Wood had to go off injured. His career
was cruelly cut short by the tragic
Munich air crash. Although he survived,
Jackie was never able to resume
playing. An Irish international who had
appeared for his country alongside his
brother Danny, the legendary Spurs
captain. Career was cut short having
suffered a fractured pelvis in the Munich
air disaster. He then ran a paper and
sweet shop, worked for a bookmaker,
became a pub landlord and went into
the print trade. He then studied to be an
accountant and kept the books for the
Greater Manchester Youth Association.
Lived in Stalybridge near Manchester,
was a regular on the after dinner circuit
until just before his death from cancer in
September 1998, aged 65.

BLEW, Horace

Appearances: 1 Goals: 0 (1905-1906)
Career: *Wrexham, Bury, Manchester
United, Man (1904-1910).* Blew played
his only game for United against
Chelsea in April 1906 after the club had
won promotion to the First Division

He was given a gold medal to mark the
success despite only appearing once
for the first team. He went on to write
match reports for the Daily Dispatch,
joined the board of Wrexham in the
1920's, worked for the agents of the
Erddig Estate and later opened a hotel.
He was elected to Wrexham council in
1919, became mayor in 1924, an
alderman three years later and in 1948
was given the freedom of the Borough.
He died in the town in February 1957,
aged 84.

BLOMQVIST, Jesper

Appearances: 38 Goals: 1 (1998-2001)
Career: *Manchester United, Everton,
Charlton Athletic (1998-2003).* The
Swedish international was signed for
£4.4 million from Italian outfit Parma to
provide cover for Ryan Giggs. He didn't
play enough games to win a
Championship winner's medal in 1999
and was an unused sub in the FA Cup
Final but he started the Champions
League Final victory over Bayern
Munich. He missed the last two seasons
of his contract with a serious knee injury
and his contract wasn't renewed. Is now
assistant manager of Hammarby and
came out of retirement to play for them
in 2010. He has also worked as a
television pundit and splits his time
between Sweden and Croatia where he
owns property.

BODAK, Peter

Appearances: 0 Goals: 0 (1982)
Career: *Coventry City, Manchester
United, Manchester City, Crewe
Alexandra, Swansea City, Walsall (1980-
1990).* A pacy right winger, was signed
in August 1982 but left for Main Road in
December the same year without
playing a first team game. Was living in
the Midlands, working as security on the
railways as well as doing stats for the
Press Association.

BOGAN, Tommy

Appearances: 33 Goals: 7 (1951-1953)
Career: *Preston North End, Manchester United, Southampton, Blackburn Rovers, Macclesfield Town (1948-1954).* He was the partner for another former Celtic player, Jimmy Delaney, on the right wing for United, but he was never assured of his place having to battle it out with Harry McShane and Cliff Birkett towards the end of his days at the club. Settled in Alderley Edge, Cheshire, after marrying Sir Matt Busby's niece, he was employed in the newspaper industry by the Daily Express and the Manchester Evening News after leaving the game. He died in September 1993, aged 73.

BOND, Ernie

Appearances: 20 Goals: 4 (1950-1952)
Career: *Preston North End, Manchester United, Carlisle United (1948-1958).* He enjoyed his best spell at United over Christmas 1951 when he scored in three games in four days, helping the club to their first post-war title, but he was sold to Carlisle the following September for £5,000. He returned to live in his native Preston and worked in a Ribble Valley Paper Mill before going to work for Baxi Heating until taking an early retirement in May 1990. Now lives in retirement.

BOSNICH, Mark

Appearances: 38 Goals: 0 (1989-92 & 1999-2001) Career: *Sydney United, Manchester United, Aston Villa, Chelsea, Central Coast Mariners, Sydney Olympic (1988-2009).* Mark was a student at Manchester Polytechnic when he made his debut as a non-contract player keeping a clean sheet against Wimbledon. But after three games in two seasons, he was unable to gain a work permit and returned home to Australia. He returned to Old Trafford in 1999 as successor to Peter Schmeichel.

He helped the club to the Premier League title in his first season. He also played a key role in the World Club Championship success but the arrival of Fabien Barthez saw him drop down the pecking order, and ended up with him leaving for Chelsea. He was banned from the game for testing positive for cocaine and appeared on "I Am A Celebrity, Get Me Out Of Here". He now plays for Australian non-league side Sydney Olympic, and works a co-commentator and football pundit on Australian television. Is also working as a players' agent.

Mark Bosnich
Photo: CamW

BOYLE, Tommy

Appearances: 17 Goals: 6 (1928-1930)
Career: *Sheffield United, Manchester United,Macclesfield Town, Northampton Town (1921-1935).* Joined United after losing his place in the Blades side, but he couldn't hold down a regular spot at Old Trafford. His longest run in the team came after Jimmy Hanson broke his leg on Christmas Day 1929. He left to became player manager of Northampton. He had a spell as manager of Midland League Scarborough before becoming a publican, north of Middlesbrough.

BRADLEY, Warren

Appearances: 66 Goals: 21 (1958-1962)
Career: *Bolton Wanderers, Manchester United, Bury, Macclesfield (1954-1966).* Joined United as an amateur post-Munich, along with Bob Hardisty and Derek Lewin. A gritty winger who by the end of his first season, scored 12 goals in 24 games and netted on his England debut, a remarkable rise to fame. He spent four years at Old Trafford but was never part of Matt Busby's long term plans and moved to Bury for £40,000. A school teacher by profession, he became headmaster of a Manchester comprehensive school before retiring. He was also chairman of the Manchester United Former Players Association. He died in Manchester in June 2007, aged 73.

BRATT, Harold

Appearances: 1 Goals: 0 (1960-1961)
Career: *Manchester United, Doncaster Rovers (1957-1963).* Joined United as a highly promising amateur at the aged of 15 following a sparkling schoolboy career. In 1956-1957 he was part of the FA Youth Cup winning side playing both legs at left half back in the 8-2 victory over West Ham. He made his only first team appearance in the shock League Cup defeat at the hands of Bradford City in November 1960.

But at the end of the same season, he was allowed to leave for Doncaster Rovers after failing to break into the team again. Joined the Greater Manchester Police after hanging up his boots until an injury caused his early retirement. Now lives in Salford.

BRAZIL, Alan

Appearances: 41 Goals: 12 (1984-1986)
Career: *Ipswich Town, Tottenham Hotspur, Manchester United, Coventry City, Queens Park Rangers (1977-1997).* Signed by United for £700,000 in August 1984 after failing to settle at White Hart Lane, but he never really had a run in the team and struggled to become a first team regular with competition from the likes of Norman Whiteside, Mark Hughes and Frank Stapleton. He was allowed to join Coventry City in a deal which brought Terry Gibson to Old Trafford. Ran a pub in Ipswich called the Black Adder after a back injury ended his career, before embarking on a media career with Talksport where he is now a popular presenter. He splits his time between a home in London's Docklands and Suffolk where he ran a horse racing club.

BRAZIL, Derek

Appearances: 2 Goals: 0 (1988-1990)
Career: *Manchester United, Oldham Athletic, Swansea City, Cardiff City, Newport County (1988-1998).* The central defender joined United in March 1986 after a successful trial. He was a regular in the Central League team but was limited to only two first team appearances because of Paul McGrath and Steve Bruce, and he eventually moved on to Cardiff City for a fee of around £85,000. Is still based in South Wales where he runs his own physical education teaching and football coaching business in the Cardiff area. He has also been manager of Haverfordwest since October 2006.

BREBNER, Grant

Appearances: 0 Goals: 0 (1994-1998)
Career: *Manchester United, Cambridge United, Reading, Stockport County (1998-2001).* An Edinburgh born midfielder who joined United from school in 1994, and a year later was a member of the FA Cup winning squad. In total, he spent four seasons in the reserve and youth teams and was released as a 21 year old, without making a first team appearance, to join Reading. After spells in Scotland with Hibs and Dundee United in 2006, he joined Melbourne Victory and has helped them to Grand Final victories in 2007 and 2009.

BREEDON, John

Appearances: 38 Goals: 0 (1935-1940)
Career: *Sheffield Wednesday, Manchester United, Burnley (1930-1946).* In his first three seasons at Old Trafford, United were promoted twice and relegated once. It wasn't until the 1938-1939 season that he managed to dislodge Tommy Breen from the first team, and then three games into his second season, League football was suspended after the outbreak of World War Two. He continued to play for United through the War years until Jack Crompton took over in peace time. Went into management with Halifax after leaving Turf Moor and scouted for Bradford City before managing Bradford Park Avenue. Based in Leeds, he scouted for the local club. He died in 1977, aged 70.

BRENNAN, Shay

Appearances: 359 Goals: 6 (1957-1970)
Career: *Manchester United (1957-1970).* Started his career in tragic circumstances in the ashes of the Munich disaster. He made his debut against Sheffield Wednesday in the first game after the crash, he scored twice on an emotionally charged night.

He was an FA Youth Cup winner in 1955, missed two FA Cup finals but won League Championship winner's medals in 1965 and 1967. He was also a member of the European Cup winning side. As the rock at the heart of Matt Busby's defence, his contribution to the club was rewarded with two testimonials. Shay went on to manage Waterford and decided to settle in the area, where he set up his own parcel courier company. He continued to live in Tramore until his death from a heart attack in June 2000, aged 63.

BRETT, Frank

Appearances: 10 Goals: 0 (1921-1922)
Career: *Manchester United, Aston Villa, Northampton Town, Brighton & Hove Albion (1921-1930).* Was only cleared to play for United by the FA after it emerged he had signed amateur forms with Aston Villa. He started his only season as full back but lost his place after six games to Charlie Retford and left, ironically, for Villa Park at the end of his only season at the club. He settled in Sussex running a coal merchants business in Hove before opening a bookmakers with his former Brighton team mate, Ernie Wilson, He lived in Chichester in retirement and died in July 1988, aged 89.

BRIGGS, Ronnie

Appearances: 11 Goals: 0 (1960-1962)
Career: *Manchester United, Swansea City, Bristol Rovers (1960-1968).* Joined United straight from school and had the misfortune to concede six goals on the debut against Leicester City. He then let in seven on his third appearance and found his chances limited afterwards by Harry Gregg and Dave Gaskell, and when United signed amateur Mike Pinner, his days at the club were numbered. He settled in Bristol, firstly in Frenchay and then Stapleton. He worked in insurance, construction and then security before his death from lung cancer in August 2008, aged 65.

Photo: Bernt Rostad

BRIGHTWELL, Stuart

Appearances: 0 Goals: 0 (1996-1998)
Career: *Manchester United, Hartlepool United (1996-1999).* Came through the youth ranks at Old Trafford but moved to Hartlepool for a season without having played a first team game. Is now a football coach at East Durham College.

BROADIS, Ivor

Appearances: 2 Goals 1
Career: *Manchester United war time guest.* He served in the RAF as a navigator and played in two games against Everton in September 1943. Scored four goals for Queen of the South in a 7-1 victory over Queens Park on Boxing Day 1959. The Queens Park scorer was one, Alex Ferguson! He has lived in Carlisle since 1955 and worked as a journalist for 45 years.

BROOMFIELD, Herbert

Appearances: 9 Goals: 0 (1907-1908)
Career: *Bolton Wanderers, Manchester United, Manchester City (1902-1910).* One of two new goalkeepers brought into the club for the 1908 title winning season but only saw action in nine games and very few reserve games, so looked for a move to Hyde Road at the end of the season. Was secretary of the Players' Union in its inception, was a landscape gardener by trade but went into business with painting and decorating in Northwich.

BROWN, Berry

Appearances: 4 Goals: 0 (1947-1948)
Career: *Manchester United, Doncaster Rovers, Hartlepools United (1947-1956).* Berry was one of six keepers on United's books. Served in the RAF during national service and was granted leave to make his league debut against Sheffield United in January 1948. He impressed in two games over Easter 1948 keeping clean sheets against Huddersfield Town and Bolton. He only made one further appearance in a 4-3 defeat against Blackpool and moved to Doncaster in January 1949, with Jack Crompton firmly first choice between the sticks at Old Trafford. He returned to his native North East and worked in a Hartlepool steelworks. He sadly died in June 2001. His son David, who played for Bury, worked at Manchester airport and now lives in Italy.

BROWN, David

(1997-1998)
Career: *Manchester United, Hull City, Torquay United, Chester City, Hereford United, Accrington Stanley, Wrexham (1997-2010).* Joined United as an apprentice and did well enough to be offered a professional contract two years later, but left within 12 months after failing to break into the first team squad. Dropped into non league football after leaving Accrington Stanley and has been playing for Wrexham in the Blue Square Premier.

BROWN, James

Appearances: 41 Goals: 17 (1932-1934)
Career: *Manchester United, Brentford, Tottenham Hotspur (1932-1937).* Was signed by United abroad an Atlantic liner after manager Scott Duncan took a tug boat out to meet it, in a bid to beat rivals to his signature. He scored on his debut against Grimsby but came into conflict with the club's management because of his support for the Players' Union, and was allowed to leave for Brentford despite his fantastic scoring record. After retiring from playing, he worked as a riveter in a Troon shipyard, a trade he learnt in the States, where he eventually returned to became head coach of Greenwich High School. He then coached Brunswick School for 22 years and the Elizabeth Falcons in the American Soccer League. He died in Berkeley Heights, New Jersey, in November 1994, aged 85.

Photo: Struway

BRUCE, Steve

Appearances: 414 Goals: 51 (1987-1996) Career: Gillingham, Norwich City, Manchester United, Birmingham City, Sheffield United (1978-1999). Signed by United for a fee of around £800,000, it is hard to believe that Steve Bruce never won a full England cap. Despite his heroic exploits for United, only 'B' team, recognition was ever gained. As well as providing solidity in defence, he had a knack of scoring vital goals. In 1990-1991, his tally of 19 including 11 penalties would have put many a striker to shame. He helped United win their first ever League Cup, captaining the side in place of Bryan Robson. Before leaving Old Trafford, he won a further three Premier League titles, three FA Cup's, three Charity Shields, A Cup Winners Cup and a Super Cup. Bruce went on to manage Sheffield United, Huddersfield Town, Wigan Athletic (twice), Crystal Palace and Birmingham City, before taking up his current position as boss of Sunderland. He is often touted as a future contender for top job at Old Trafford.

BRYANT, Billy

Appearances: 160 Goals: 44 (1934-1940) Career: Wolverhampton Wanderers, Wrexham, Manchester United, Bradford City (1931-1946). Bryant joined United from Wrexham in October 1934 in a joint deal with Tommy Bamford, and became a consistent performer for the whole of his time at the club. He won a Division Two Championship winner's medal and was first choice inside right at the outbreak of World War Two. He played through the war years and had one season at Bradford City after peace was declared. Worked as a pressure tester for Metro-Vickers during the War before working for ICI in their Trafford Park stores in his post-playing days. He eventually retired back to his native north-east and died in Durham on Christmas day 1975 at the age of 62.

Guess who?
Photo: N.VTM

BUCHAN, George

Appearances: 4 Goals: 0 (1973-1974)
Career: *Manchester United, Bury (1973-1976)*. The brother of Martin, he moved South from Aberdeen but only made four substitute appearances in the autumn of 1973, and he left the club when United were relegated from Division One at the end of that season. A school teacher by profession, he worked in Oldham during his stay in Lancashire.

Photo: Sporting Memorabilia

BUCHAN, Martin

Appearances: 456 Goals: 4 (1972-1983)
Career: *Manchester United, Oldham Athletic (1972-1983)*. Martin Buchan was a defender of great class and possessed natural leadership ability. He was captain of his home town club, Aberdeen by the age of 20 and voted Scottish Player of the Year only two years later. In March 1972, Frank O'Farrell paid the Dons a then club record fee of £125,000 to add the Scotsman's talents to the back four and it wasn't long before he had also claimed the skipper's arm-band. Martin led United back into Division One in 1974-1975 and to three FA Cup finals in four years.

He also gained a winner's medal in 1977. Moved to Oldham Athletic in August 1983 but was forced to retire through injury in October 1984. Briefly became manager at Burnley. Now lives in Sale and after leaving Turf Moor, took employment as a promotions manager for PUMA for many years. Is now an executive for the PFA.

BUCKLE, Ted

Appearances: 24 Goals: 7 (1945-1950)
Career: *Manchester United, Everton, Exeter City (1945-1957)*. Spotted by the legendary Louis Rocca while playing for the Royal Navy during World War Two, he was signed by United at the end of the conflict. Despite scoring four goals in seven games during his first season, he was never able to get a run of games with Charlie Mitten and Jimmy Delaney in front of him in the United pecking order. He stayed as a fringe player until his transfer to Everton. He worked in a timber yard, with a view to becoming a commercial traveller. He died in Manchester in June 1990, aged 65.

BUCKLEY, Major Frank

Appearances: 3 Goals: 0 (1906-1907)
Career: *Aston Villa, Brighton & Hove Albion, Manchester United, Manchester City, Birmingham City, Derby County, Bradford City, Norwich City (1902-1920)*. He spent one season at Old Trafford as understudy to Charlie Roberts and left after only making three appearances. He went on to rise to the rank of Major, serving in the Football Battalion during the Great War. Became a legendary manager with Wolves between 1927 and 1944 after cutting his teeth in management with Norwich City and Blackpool. Had worked as a salesman in between his first two jobs, he later had spells in charge of Notts County, Hull City, Leeds United and Walsall.

BULLIMORE, Wayne

Appearances: 0 Goals: 0 (1988-1991)
Career: *Manchester United, Barnsley, Stockport County, Scunthorpe United, Bradford City, Doncaster Rovers, Peterborough United, Scarborough (1991-1998).* Spent three years at Old Trafford as a trainee but wasn't offered a professional contract and left the club to join Barnsley. After a long spell in non-league football, he is now chief executive of Barnsley's Sports and Community Education trust. He also coaches the Under-10s side in the Barnsley Academy.

BURGESS, Herbert

Appearances: 52 Goals: 0 (1906-1910)
Career: *Glossop, Manchester City, Manchester United (1900-1910).* A full back who saw his career cut short by a serious knee injury, he was one of a host of City players to move to United in December 1906. He won a League Championship medal in 1908, only to have to quit the game within two years. He ran a pub near Old Trafford after retiring before embarking on a coaching career that took in Hungary, Spain, Austria, Denmark and Sweden. He died in Manchester in July 1954, aged 70.

BURKE, Ronald

Appearances: 28 Goals: 16 (1946-1949)
Career: *Manchester United, Huddersfield Town, Rotherham United, Exeter City (1946-1957).* Spotted by Jimmy Murphy playing for the RAF in Italy, and the two became friends. He signed as a professional in August 1946 but couldn't hold down a regular place in the first team with the likes of John Morris, Arthur Rowley and Stan Pearson preferred. Despite his goal scoring record, Burke was sold to Huddersfield Town in June 1949 after handing in a number of transfer requests. Worked as a probationer nurse at a Watford mental hospital before the War.

After hanging up his boots, he was a progress section leader for Rolls Royce in Watford before his death in December 2003, aged 82.

BURNS, Francis

Appearances: 121 Goals: 6 (1965-1973)
Career: *Manchester United, Southampton, Preston North End (1965-1981).* He moved south of the border in 1965 and his six years at United would have been more productive had it not been for repeated injury problems. He was a regular starter until losing his place to Shay Brennan. He played the first seven games in United's European Cup winning campaign, he was a cultured defender but was sold to Southampton for £50,000. Francis emigrated to Australia in 1987 and went on to run dry cleaning and industrial cleaning businesses in Perth. He now works for a local radio station.

Fabien Barthez!
Photo: N.VTM

Fancy coming to an Eric Cantona party? *Photo: chas2112*

BUTT, Len

Appearances: 11 Goals: 8
Career: *Manchester United war time
guest.* One of the first guest players
used by United at the start of WW2, a
clinical finisher he made his debut in a
defeat to Liverpool in November 1939.
Managed Mossley and Macclesfield
whilst working as a stonemason, he
passed away in 1994 aged 83, after a
series of strokes.

BUTT Nicky

*Appearances: 387 Goals: 26 (1992-
2004)* Career: *Manchester United,
Birmingham City, Newcastle United
(1992-2010).* Another member of
United's 1992 FA Youth Cup winning
side who progressed to the very top of
his profession. He was drafted into the
first team to partner Roy Keane after
Paul Ince was sold to Inter in the
summer of 1995. He spent a total of 12
seasons in the first team squad, winning
six Premier League titles, three FA Cups,
three Community Shields, a Champions
League and an Intercontinental Cup. But
faced with increasingly limited chances,
he handed in a transfer request and was
sold to Newcastle United for £2.5 million
in July 2004. Butt decided to retire after
helping Newcastle United win the
Championship title in May 2010 and has
shown an interest to move into coaching.

BYRNE, Roger

Appearances: 245 Goals:17
Career: *Manchester United (1951-1957).*
Byrne joined United at the age of 20,
went on to captain the 'Busby Babes'
and to win 33 England caps, before he
and his team mates were struck down in
the Munich air disaster of 1958. He had
already won three League titles and at
28, he had the best years of his career
ahead of him but is still remembered
today as one of United's greatest ever
captains because of his ability to inspire
and lead his players. Amazingly, during
his national service in the RAF, he wasn't
considered to be good enough to play

for the football team and ended up
playing rugby. Roger's funeral was held
in Flixton parish church and his body
was cremated.

CAMPBELL, Fraizer

Appearances: 4 Goals: 0 (2006-2009)
Career: *Manchester United, Hull City,
Tottenham Hotspur, Sunderland (2006-
2010).* A striker who was a prolific goal
scorer for the youth team and reserves,
progressing into the first team squad.
He was even sent on loan to Spurs as a
makeweight in the deal that brought
Dimitar Berbatov to Old Trafford. Sir
Alex Ferguson accepted a bid from
Sunderland in July 2009.

CANTONA, Eric

*Appearances: 185 Goals: 82 (1992-
1997)* Career: *Leeds United,
Manchester United (1992-1997).* A
shock £1.2 million signing after moves
for other players failed and Leeds had
enquired about Denis Irwin. He settled
quickly and was inspirational in the
winning of the inaugural Premier League
crown, the club's first title since 1967. in
doing so, became the only player to win
back to back titles with different clubs.
The next season United did the double
but his third season was wrecked by his
infamous Kung Fu kick on a Crystal
Palace fan. He returned to action after
an eight month ban in October 1995 and
scored on his comeback against
Liverpool. At the end of the season, he
had helped United to a second double.
He took his tally of titles with United to
four in five years in 1996-1997 but then
surprised the football world when he
announced his retirement aged 30. King
Eric then competed in beach soccer
until 2008, playing for and being the
captain of the French international beach
soccer team. He has since become a
television, film and stage actor, notably
appearing in the 2009 film "Looking for
Eric", about a fanatical Manchester
United fan who suffers hallucinations of
Cantona.

Photo: Sporting Memorabilia

CANTWELL, Noel

Appearances: 146 Goals: 8 (1960-1967)
Career: West Ham United, Manchester United (1952-1967). His performances for West Ham prompted United to pay £29,500 (a record for a full back) to prise him away from Upton Park in 1960. Having more than repaid his fee with solid displays in the red number two shirt, he reminded many at Old Trafford of Johnny Carey with his gentlemanly approach to the game. In his seven years at old trafford, he played in the successful 1963 FA Cup winning side. He retired in 1967 after only playing a handful of games during the march to the title. Tipped by many to succeed Matt Busby, he left the club to take charge of Coventry City. After Coventry, he managed in the Republic of Ireland and the New England Teamen in America. Until his retirement in 1999, Cantwell took on the New Inn pub, close to another of his managerial stop-offs, Peterborough United, where he was twice manager and had also served as general manager. He lost a long battle to cancer in September 2005, aged 73.

CAPE, Jack

Appearances: 60 Goals: 18 (1933-1936)
Career: Carlisle United, Newcastle United, Manchester United, Queens Park Rangers, Carlisle United (1929-1947). The scorer of the goal against Millwall that maintained United's Second Division status in 1933-1934 to fully repay his £2,000 transfer fee. He then played 17 games two seasons later when they were League Champions, before leaving for a stint in West London with Queens Park Rangers. Briefly held the post of reserve team trainer at Carlisle United but he had worked as an electrician before turning professional and returned to the trade during the war and when he retired.

CAREY, Johnny

Appearances: 344 Goals: 18 (1937-1953) Career: Manchester United (1937-1953). Another discovery by the great Louis Rocca, he was signed for £250, while still only aged 17, and initially faced stiff competition from Stan Pearson. He went on to play every position except outside left and even played one game in goal against Sunderland in 1953. In 1948 he became the first Irishman to lift the FA Cup and then four years later was an integral part of the League title winning squad. He played for both Northern Ireland and the Republic in a glittering career and was voted 'Player of The Year' in 1949. Managed Blackburn Rovers, Everton and was once sacked in the back of the taxi, which coined the phrase "taxi for xxxxxx". He guided Leyton Orient into the first division, then managed Nottingham Forest and returned to Blackburn for a second spell before becoming a scout. He undertook this role for United until 1985 while also working at the Borough Treasurer's office in Sale. Carey died in August 1995, aged 76.

JOHN CAREY
Manchester United and Ireland
John uses craft instead of speed, and brains instead of brawn, to beat his opponent. He has played in five positions for Eire and in all except goal for the United. He captains both club and country and is perhaps the outstanding

Photo: David Mullen

CAREY, Brian

Appearances: 0 Goals: 0 (1989-1993)
Career: *Manchester United, Wrexham, Leicester City, Wrexham (1989-2007).*
Signed from Cork City in August 1989, he spent a total of four seasons at Old Trafford without breaking into the first team squad. At the age of 25 he was released on a free transfer. Had a spell as Wrexham manager in 2007 following the departure of Denis Smith, and then caretaker boss. Is now Dean Saunders' assistant at the Racecourse Ground.

CARALON, Joe

Appearances: 66 Goals: 0 (1958-1961)
Career: *Manchester United, Brighton (1958-1962).* Came from the same Home Farm club as Johnny Giles after being discovered by Billy Behan. He made his way through the ranks converting and was a regular in the first team until the arrival of Noel Cantwell. . He worked as a window cleaner when he first gave up full-time football before joining a welding equipment and protective clothing company, and then becoming a milkman in Maidstone.

CARRICK, Willie

Appearances: 0 Goals:0 (1970-1972)
Career: *Manchester United. Luton Town (1972-1973).* A Dublin born keeper, joined United in September 1970. He spent two years as a professional at the club without playing a first team game. Left to play four games for Luton, then managed Witham Town. Has settled in Essex where he has worked for Proctor and Gamble in Thurrock for 30 years.

CARROLL, Roy

Appearances: 72 Goals: 0 (2001-2005)
Career: *Hull City, Wigan A, Manchester United, West Ham, Derby C (1995-2009).* United paid a fee of around £2.5 million and he immediately faced stiff competition from Fabien Barthez but won a Premier League winner's medal in his second season at Old Trafford, and then won an FA Cup winner's medal in May 2004 when he came on as a late substitute for Tim Howard. He was released at the end of the following season however, after refusing to sign a new contract because he wasn't assured of being first choice. Was treated for gambling and alcohol addictions, he has been playing for Odense BK in Denmark since August 2009.

CASPER, Chris

Appearances: 7 Goals: 0 (1993-98)
Career: *Manchester United, AFC Bournemouth, Swindon Town, Reading (1993-2000).* He joined United as a trainee in 1991 making his debut three years later in a League Cup tie at Port Vale, but he was never considered to be a first team regular despite being an England youth team captain and was allowed to leave the club to join Reading. Casper was forced to retire from football in 2000, aged 24, after suffering a double leg fracture. He went on to coach Team Bath before becoming Bury's youth team coach. In 2005, aged 29, he was appointed manager of Bury, making him the youngest manager in the League. He has since worked for Bradford City as youth team manager, and then assistant manager of Grimsby Town. In June , he returned to Old Trafford as a youth coach.

CATTERICK, Harry

Appearances: 15 Goals 10.
Career: *Manchester United war time guest.* He played the second half of the 1941-1944 season and the first games of the following season, scoring in his final game for the club against Blackburn Rovers. Became a legendary manager with Everton leading them to two League titles. He died of a heart attack less than an hour after watching Everton play Ipswich in an FA Cup quarter final in March 1985. He was 65.

CHADWICK, Luke

Appearances: 29 Goals: 2 (1999-2004)
Career: *Manchester United, Reading, Burnley, West Ham United, Stoke City, Norwich City, Milton Keynes Dons (1999-2009).* An England Under-21 international winger who made his way through the United academy ranks into the first team squad. He was a regular squad member but was handed a free transfer in 2004 and joined West Ham United. He is currently at Milton Keynes Dons after a successful loan spell.

CHALMERS, Stewart

Appearances: 35 Goals: 1 (1932-1934)
Career: *Manchester United (1932-1934).* Became one of several Scotsman signed by A. Scott Duncan when he took over at the club, didn't score the number of goals fitting of his talents, and the signings of Neil Dewar and Ernie Hine forced him out of the door and back up to Scotland. An accountant by profession, he worked in Scotland after hanging up his boots.

Photo: Ray Haslam

CHARLTON, Sir Bobby

Appearances: 758 Goals: 249 (1956-1973) Career: *Manchester United, Preston North End (1956-1974).*
Arguably Manchester United's greatest servant, Sir Bobby has been part of the club's ups and downs for over forty years. Even taking into account brief spells at Preston and Wigan at the tail end of his playing career, there is no doubt that his knighthood was bestowed for services to one establishment in particular, his beloved Manchester United Football Club. From the moment he first ventured to the city from his native north-east, it was obvious that here was a star in the making. Within a year, young Bobby had signed professional terms and started out on a career that would take in over 750 games. Having survived both the horror of the Munich accident as well as the terrible trauma that followed, thankfully highs were a plenty. 106 England caps can be proudly displayed alongside winner's medals from FA Cup, European Cup and World Cup victories. On an individual basis, he also added the title of Footballer of the Year, European Footballer of the Year, an OBE in 1969 and finally the right to be called 'Sir' in 1994. For the fans, he has provided a lifetime of memories: not only great goals, of which he scored over 300, but tremendous dedication and skill; as well as in later years, the unique picture of his remaining strands of hair flapping in the wind as he set off on a foray into an opponent's danger area before unleashing one of his famous rocket shots! He had a spell as manager of Preston, then built up several businesses from travel, jewellery and ran a global soccer school. He has been a United director since 1994, and has been an ambassador for several bids to bring sporting events to England from the Commonwealth Games, Olympics Games and the World Cup.

The Cup Final. Big threat to Bolton was Manchester United's inside forward Bobby Charlton, here tackled by Bolton's international left-back Tommy Banks. United fought well but went down 2—0, Nat Lofthouse scoring both Bolton's goals.

Photo: David Mullen

CHILTON, Allenby

Appearances: 390 Goals: 3 (1939-1955)
Career: *Liverpool, Manchester United, Grimsby Town (1938-1956)*. A dominating central defender who was tough enough to give up soccer for a while to try his hand at boxing. Played his first League match just before the War, then had a frustrating wait during which time he sustained a wartime injury. However, by the time hostilities had finished, he had established himself as a first team regular, a position he managed to maintain, well into the 1950s. In 1955, with two England caps and over 350 United appearances under his belt, the Geordie man moved a little closer to home when he took over as player manager at Grimsby Town. Chilton later went on to manage Wigan Athletic and Hartlepool United. He left the game to run a shop for five years and then worked in a steelworks for 14 years. He died in June 1996, aged 77, after retiring to Sunderland in 1981.

CHISNALL, Phil

Appearances: 47 Goals: 10 (1961-1964)
Career: *Manchester United, Liverpool, Southend United, Stockport County (1959-1972)*. A talented youngster, broke into United's star studded forward line after impressing for the reserves, only to lose his place to Graham Moore in 1963-1964 when he started the campaign as first choice inside right. Matt Busby had his doubts and he never really had another extended run in the first team. He was sold to Liverpool for £25,000 in April 1964 and remains the last player transferred between Anfield and Old Trafford. He ran several betting shops until taking a pre-retirement job as a factory processor in Trafford Park.

CLARK, Jonathan

Appearances: 1 Goals: 0 (1976-1977)
Career: *Manchester United, Derby County, Preston North End, Bury,*
Carlisle United, Morecombe (1975-1989). A midfielder who made his league debut as a sub against Sunderland in November 1976, failed to break into the first team again and was sold to Derby County for £50,000 in September 1978. He became a licensee and runs the Clarence Hotel in Blackpool.

CLAYTON, Gordon

Appearances: 2 Goals: 0 (1956-1957)
Career: *Manchester United, Tranmere Rovers (1953-1961)*. Joined United on the same day as his school boy friend, Duncan Edwards, a member of United's outstanding 1953 FA Youth Cup winning team. He only made two first team appearances against Wolves and West Bromwich Albion, but with Ray Wood as first choice keeper, he left for Tranmere along with Bobby Harrop. He represented the club as eight funerals for victims of the Munich air crash. He joined the police force after leaving Tranmere but then returned to United as assistant chief scout in the early 70s. He then went to scout for Derby and was assistant manager of Burnley for a spell. His career ended in non league football with Cheadle Town and Northwich Victoria, where he was assistant manager to his close friend Sammy McIlroy at the time of his death in Stretford in September 1991.

CLEGG, Mike

Appearances: 24 Goals: 0 (1996-2003)
Career: *Manchester United, Ipswich Town, Wigan Athletic, Oldham Athletic (1995-2004)*. A member of the 1995 FA Youth Cup winning team, he played in two Premier League winning campaigns but never enough games to qualify for a winner's medal, and after failing to win a regular place in the side, he was allowed to leave the club on a free transfer. Hung up his boots at the age of 27, he is now at Sunderland where he works as strength and conditioning coach.

CLEMPSON, Frank

Appearances: 15 Goals: 2 (1948-1953)
Career: *Manchester United, Stockport County, Chester City (1948-1961).* A Salford born striker who could also play wing half, joined United as an amateur in March 1948. He was still only 19 when he got his first team chance in February 1950, after an injury to Tommy Brogan. The 1951-1952 Championship winning season saw him play eight games and score two goals. But after only a handful of appearances in five years, he moved to Stockport. Became player manager of Hyde United to finish his career. Sadly died in Worsley, in December 1970 aged just 40, after suffering ill-health for a number of years.

COCKBURN, Henry

Appearances: 275 Goals: 4 (1946-1955)
Career: *Manchester United, Bury (1946-1955).* A giant in style and ability but it wasn't until he was tried at half back that he realised his true potential. He won an FA Cup winner's medal in 1948 and then a League Championship four years later but requested a move and left after losing his place to Duncan Edwards. After working as coach at Oldham Athletic, then Huddersfield Town, he joined Mitre Sports where he worked until retiring to Ashton-Under-Lyne, the town of his birth. He died on 2nd February 2004, aged 82.

Photo: Egghead06

COLE, Andrew

Appearances: 272 Goals: 121 (1994-2002) Career: *Arsenal, Fulham, Bristol C, Newcastle U, Manchester United, Blackburn R, Fulham, Manchester C, Portsmouth, Birmingham C, Sunderland, Burnley, Nottingham F (1989-2008).* Many critics questioned why Sir Alex Ferguson paid a British record £6 million, plus Keith Gillespie to Newcastle in January 1995, to land Cole but he soon answered why with 12 goals in his first 18 games for the club. His second season at Old Trafford saw him win the double but United were still willing to offer him to Blackburn Rovers in a £12m bid to land Alan Shearer, who opted for Newcastle United instead. He then returned from breaking his legs to score the title winning goal at Anfield. He went onto win a total of five Premier League titles, two FA Cup and Charity Shields, a UEFA Champions League before being sold to Blackburn for £8 million following the arrival of Ruud van Nistelrooy. Cole has worked as a coach at Milton Keynes Dons, and currently trains forwards at Huddersfield Town. He also works with several charities.

COLLETT, Ben

Appearances: 0 Goals: 0 (2002-2006) Career: *Manchester United (2002-2006).* Signed on at United as a trainee in 2001 and progressed through the youth teams, and in 2002-2003, was named Jimmy Murphy Young Player of the Year after helping United to an FA Youth Cup Final win over Middlesbrough. A week later he played a reserve team game against the same opposition and suffered a break to his leg. In 2006, he was released by United after failing to play a first team game. After spells in New Zealand, he was forced to quit the game as a result of the injuries received and after launching a legal action, he was awarded an initial £4.2 million in compensation. Is now studying English at Leeds University.

COLMAN, Eddie

Appearances: 108 Goals: 2 (1953-57)
Career: Manchester United (1955-1957).
Former Army rat catcher and United
youth team player, he was part of the
United side which won three successive
FA Youth Cups. Eddie, known as
'snakehips' or 'swivelhips', was an
integral part of the Busby Babes. He
struck up an immediate understanding
with Duncan Edwards, picked up two
championship medals and played in the
1957 FA Cup final before dying in the
Munich air crash. He was still only 21
years old at the time. He is buried in
Weaste Cemetery in Salford alongside
his parents.

CONNAUGHTON, John

Appearances: 3 Goals: 0 (1966-1972)
*Career: Manchester United, Halifax
Town, Torquay United, Sheffield United,
Port Vale (1966-1980).* Spent seven
years at Old Trafford but it was spent in
the shadow of Alex Stepney and Jimmy
Rimmer. He was recalled from a loan
spell at Torquay United to make his
debut against Sheffield United at Bramall
Lane in April 1972, giving an assured
display. He moved to the South
Yorkshire in October the same year for
£15,000. He became a millionaire from
running a highly successful waste paper
business.

CONNELL, Thomas

Appearances: 2 Goals: 0 (1978-1982)
Career: Manchester United (1978-1982).
The hard tackling full back only made
two appearances as deputy for Stewart
Houston against Bolton Wanderers in
December 1978, and then the game
against Liverpool on Boxing Day. He
never broke into the first team again
despite being a regular for the Central
League team and was sold by Ron
Atkinson to Glentoran for £37,000. Is
now back living in his native Newry.

Photo: Sporting Memorabilia

CONNELLY, John

*Appearances: 113 Goals: 35 (1964-
1966) Career: Burnley, Manchester
United, Blackburn Rovers, Bury (1956-
1972).* When he joined United, it was
suggested that he was past his best but
proved to be an instant success winning
his second League Championship. An
ever present, weighing in with 15 goals,
his second season saw the club finish
ninth and reach the semi-finals of the
European Cup. He was sold to
Blackburn Rovers for £40,000 months
after appearing for England in the
opening game of the 1966 World Cup
Finals. Became the owner of a fish and
chip shop called Connelly's Plaice near
Nelson, he has now retired and travels
the world. In 2009 his contribution to the
1966 World Cup victory was finally
rewarded when the Government
decided that every member of the
squad should receive a cup winners'
medal, not just the eleven players left on
the pitch at the end of the final.

CONNOR, Ted
Appearances: 15 Goals: 2 (1909-1911)
Career: *Manchester United, Sheffield United, Bury, Exeter City, Rochdale, Chesterfield (1909-1921).* Found his first team chances limited by Billy Meredith and George Wall, scored his first goal for the club in the last game at Bank Street, Clayton, and then left for Sheffield United in a £750 deal. He scouted for United and worked in the Old Trafford offices for many years.

COOKE, Terry
Appearances: 8 Goals: 1 (1994-1999)
Career: *Manchester U, Sunderland, Birmingham C, Wrexham, Manchester C, Wigan Athletic, Sheffield Wed, Grimsby T, Sheffield Wed.* Came through the ranks at Old Trafford scoring the penalty that won the 1995 FA Youth Cup. Made his league debut against Bolton in the same season. Tipped for a bright future at the club but had the misfortune to want to play on the right side of midfield, the same position as his former youth team pal, David Beckham. Had several spells out on loan before being sold to City for £1million in March 1999. After being released by Wednesday, he headed to the MLS where he played for Colorado Rapids for four seasons before he was freed, and has played for North Queensland Fury since 2009.

COPE, Ronnie
Appearances: 106 Goals: 2 (1951-1961)
Career: *Manchester United, Luton Town (1951-1963).* Former schoolboy international who signed pro terms in 1951 but he had to be content with a supporting role. He joined Luton Town in 1961 for £10,000 bringing to an end his ten year association with the club. He hails from Crewe where he now lives in retirement. He spent 14 years at Northwich Victoria as a player and in management before going to work for Prudential Insurance for 21 years until retiring.

Photo: brizzlechris

COPPELL, Steve
Appearances: 396 Goals: 70 (1974-1983) Career: *Tranmere Rovers, Manchester United (1973-1982).* A Liverpool born winger who joined in February 1975 from Tranmere Rovers for what proved to be a bargain fee of £60,000. The former Liverpool University student took over from Willie Morgan on United's right wing in their Second Division Championship season, and for the next eight seasons as first choice, playing 205 consecutive matches between 15th January 1977 and 7th November 1981. A FA Cup winner in 1977, forced to retire through injury in 1983 thanks to a serious knee injury he suffered on international duty. Went into management at Crystal Palace only to resign in 1993 and became Chief Executive of the Football League Managers Association, a post that he held until March 1995. Returned to Selhurst Park as technical director. Has also managed Brentford, Brighton and Reading, he took charge of Bristol City but quit and announced he was retiring after just two games in August 2010.

Eric Cantona Mosaic *Photo: dullhunk*

Pat Crerand with Mike Summerbee   *Photo: visitmanchester*

COTON, Tony

Appearances: 0 Goals: 0 (1996)
Career: *Birmingham City, Hereford U, Watford, Manchester City, Manchester United, Sunderland, Hereford United (1978-2004).* Transferred for a record £500,000 between the Manchester giants but never played a first team game for United and moved to Sunderland after only six months at Old Trafford. Coton became Manchester United's goalkeeping coach, but stepped down in 2007 due to a knee injury that prevented him from taking part in training sessions. He now works as a players' agent.

COYNE, Peter

Appearances: 2 Goals: 1 (1975-1976)
Career: *Manchester United, Crewe Alexandra, Swindon Town, Aldershot (1975-1989).* An England school boy international, was a prolific scorer for the youth team but he never realised his true potential at first team level despite scoring on his debut against Leicester City at Filbert Street in April 1976 and his contract was terminated the following March. He is now back living in the Manchester area working in security at the airport and coaching in local schools.

CRERAND, Pat

Appearances: 397 Goals: 15 (1962-1971) Career: *Manchester United (1962-1971).* Became the cornerstone of many a famous United victory following his £56,00 capture from Celtic in February 1963, and three months later he helped the club to win the FA Cup. Hard working and always in the thick of the action, he played vital roles in winning two League Championship titles in 1965 and then 1967, as well as the famous European Cup Final victory over Benfica at Wembley in 1968.
To this day he remains fiercely loyal to the United cause. Joined the coaching staff at United, later becoming their Assistant Manager until 1975.

Managed Northampton from July 1976 until January 1977. On leaving football be became a public relations officer to a Manchester engineering company. Became landlord at the Park Hotel, Altrincham. Today he appears regularly on MUTV and was a pundit on the phone-in show "Crerand and Bower...In Extra Time" until Steve Bower left in 2007.

CROMPTON, John

Appearances: 212 Goals: 0 (1945-1956)
Career: *Manchester United (1945-1956).* Former inside forward who switched to playing in goal before he joined United during the war, he had spells with Newton Heath Loco and Goslings FC. Capable, brave and reliable, he was United's first choice between the sticks after making his debut against Grimsby until the arrival of Reg Allen in June 1950. He won his place back only to lose it to Ray Wood. An FA Cup winner in 1948, he was a Division One runner up for three consecutive seasons. Later coached at Luton Town, Preston North End and Barrow as well as returning to Old Trafford in 1958 to help out following the Munich air disaster. In all, he had three spells on the United coaching staff. He lived in Tenerife for a spell, worked as Governor and football coach to the Tenerife English Education Centre and now lives in retirement in Oldham.

CROOKS, Garth

Appearances: 7 Goals: 2 (1983-1984)
Career: *Stoke City, Tottenham Hotspur, Manchester United, West Bromwich Albion, Charlton Athletic (1975-1990).* The striker was signed on loan from Spurs and made his debut against Norwich City in November 1983, scored his two goals against Ipswich Town and Notts County before being recalled to White Hart Lane. Now works as a pundit/reporter for BBC TV, he was Chairman of the Institute of Professional Sport, and is on the board of the North West London school Capital City Academy.

CROSSLEY, Mark

Appearances: 0 Goals: 0 (1990)
Career: Nottingham Forest, Manchester United, Millwall, Middlesbrough, Stoke City, Fulham, Sheffield Wednesday, Oldham Athletic, Chesterfield (1987-2010). Joined United on loan from Nottingham Forest but was never called upon to play in the first team before returning to the City Ground. Crossley took his first step into coaching whilst with Oldham Athletic, when he was signed as player-goalkeeping coach. He is now goalkeeping coach for Chesterfield whilst also still registered as a player to provide back up for the club's first choice keeper.

CROWTHER, Stan

Appearances: 20 Goals: 0 (1957-1959)
Career: Aston Villa, Manchester United, Chelsea, Brighton (1955-1961). Was an £18,000 signing by United in the wake of the Munich air crash, he joined just one hour and sixteen minutes before the FA Cup tie against Sheffield Wednesday and even though he had already played in the competition, he was given special dispensation to play. He helped the club reach the final. He wasn't in the club's long term plans and was sold to Chelsea for £10,000. Moved back to his native Black Country after quitting through disillusionment. Became a senior foreman at the Armitage Shanks factory in Wolverhampton until retirement.

CRUYFF, Jordi

Appearances: 58 Goals: 8 (1996-2002)
Career: Ajax, Barcelona, Manchester United, Celta Vigo, Alaves, Espanyol, Metalurh Donetsk, Valletta (1991-2010). Signed from Barcelona for a fee of £1.4 million, his debut was overshadowed by David Beckham scoring from the half-way line against Wimbledon. He scored on his second and third appearances for the club but then suffered a knee injury which became an all too familiar story for his stay at the club. He was at Old Trafford for three title wins but only gained one winner's medal in his first season because of his poor injury record. He moved back to Spain to join Alaves in a bid to kick-start his once promising career. He took his first steps in management as the assistant manager of Maltese club Valletta, but has since taken charge of AEK Larnaca. He also has a fashion business with the Cruyff clothing brand.

CULKIN, Nick

Appearances: 1 Goals: 0 (1995-2002)
Career: York City, Manchester United, Hull City, Bristol Rovers, Queens Park Rangers (1994-2005). Nick was signed for £250,000 despite never having played a game for York and is in United's history books for having the shortest team career when he replaced Raimond van der Gouw for the final 80 seconds of a 2-1 victory at Arsenal in 1999. After being forced to retire in 2005 through a knee injury, he came out of retirement in August 2010 to play for Evo-Stick Division One North club, Radcliffe Borough.

CUNNINGHAM, Laurie

Appearances: 5 Goals: 1 (1982-1983)
Career: Leyton Orient, West Bromwich Albion, Manchester United, Leicester City, Wimbledon (1974-1987). Signed by United boss Ron Atkinson, who had been his mentor at previous club West Bromwich Albion, on loan from Real Madrid. He made an attempt to break back into the English game but the move wasn't a success and the magic that was once present at the Hawthorns appeared to have gone and he was allowed to return to Spain. He was sadly killed in a car crash in Madrid in July 1989, aged only 33, while playing with Rayo Vallencano.

CURRAN, Colin
Career: *Manchester United (1964-65).*
A highly talented full back who was
playing in Australia when he paid his
own way to Old Trafford in August 1965,
and stayed for six months. He improved
dramatically by the time he returned
home. In 1970, he was part of the
Australia team who played a touring
United team. A member of the
Australian 1974 World Cup squad, he
now lives in Eleebana, New South Wales.

CURTIS, John
Appearances: *19 Goals: 0 (1995-2000)*
Career: *Manchester United, Barnsley,
Blackburn R, Sheffield U, Leicester City,
Portsmouth, Preston North End. (19??-
20??).* John was still in his last year at
school when he was an FA Youth Cup
winner in 1995, and was tipped for a big
future in the game but he couldn't get a
regular game at Old Trafford. Graeme
Souness took him to Ewood Park in the
summer of 2000 for £1.5 million, after
three seasons in the professional ranks
at Old Trafford. Was released by
Northampton in May 2010 but two
months later signed a one year deal to
play in Australia for Gold Coast United.

DALTON, Paul
Appearances: *0 Goals: 0 (1988-1989)*
Career: *Manchester U, Hartlepool U,
Plymouth A, Huddersfield T, Carlisle U
(1988-2000).* Signed for United as youth
team player in 1988 from non-league
Brandon United. But was sold to
Hartlepool for £20,000 a year later.
Coached at Middlesbrough's academy
and teaches at Darlington College.

DALY, Gerry
Appearances: *142 Goals: 32 (1973-
1977)* Career: *Manchester U, Derby C,
Coventry C, Leicester C, Birmingham
C, Shrewsbury T, Stoke C, Doncaster R
(1973-1988).* Ace penalty taker who
only missed one of his 17 attempts in a
United shirt. A successful import from
Dublin club Bohemians for a bargain
£20,000, experienced relegation, but
helped gain promotion at the first
attempt. He played in two FA Cup Finals
getting a winner's medal in 1977 then
lost his place to Jimmy Greenhoff before
falling out with Tommy Docherty. He left
for Derby in a £170,000 deal. Ironically
the pair linked up again at the Baseball
Ground. Was manager of Telford United
but is now a businessman in Derby.

Munich Memorial *Photo: Gordon Flood*

DAVENPORT, Peter

Appearances: 106 Goals: 26 (1985-1989) Career: *Nottingham Forest, Manchester United, Middlesbrough, Sunderland (1982-1993)*. Cost United £570,000 in March 1986 and he failed to find the net in his first ten games. He was then the club's leading scorer in his first full season at Old Trafford with 14 goals to his name. He was a first team regular until Sir Alex Ferguson, brought Mark Hughes - the man he was signed to replace - back to the club and within months, was sold to Middlesbrough. Went into management with Macclesfield, Bangor, Colwyn Bay and Southport. In May 2010 Davenport was named assistant manager of Bradford Park Avenue. He is also a coarse angling instructor.

DAVIES, Alan

Appearances: 10 Goals: 1 (1981-1984) Career: *Manchester United, Newcastle United, Swansea City, Bradford City, Swansea City (1981-1991)*. Almost an unknown when he played for United in the 1983 Cup final, after just playing a handful of first team games but it appeared that it was going to be the launch pad for his career, only for him to suffer a broken ankle and torn ligaments in a pre-season match. He came back and scored in the UEFA Cup semi-final against Juventus but he was only at Old Trafford for another season before being sold to Newcastle United, in July 1985 for £50,000. He was sadly found dead in his car near his home on the Gower Coast, in February 1992, aged only 30. He was thought to have been suffering from depression.

DAVIES, Ron

Appearances: 10 Goals: 0 (1974-1975) Career: *Chester C, Luton T, Norwich C, Southampton, Portsmouth, Manchester U, Millwall (1959-1975)*. Sadly, the best days of Davies were well behind him when Tommy Docherty brought him to Old Trafford for £25,000, and he wasn't the same player who scored four goals for Southampton against United in 1969. He couldn't break into the starting line up and was he used off the subs bench in the ten games that he played. Became a demolition worker for a while after retiring in 1975, and also proved that he had talent with his hands as well as his feet by selling art sketches, including portraits of players. He then moved to Los Angeles, then Florida where he coached at local schools. He is now resident in Albuquerque, New Mexico, where he is working on a construction site, living in a motor home.

DAVIES, Simon

Appearances: 20 Goals: 1 (1993-1997) Career: *Manchester United, Exeter City, Huddersfield Town, Luton Town, Macclesfield Town, Rochdale, Chester City (1992-2007)*. A team mate of David Beckham and Gary Neville in United's 1992 FA Youth Cup winning side, scored his only goal for the club in the Champions League but he never held down a regular first team place and was sold to Luton Town for £150,000. Davies briefly managed Chester City in a caretaker role in 2007, before taking up the post on a permanent position a year later. In 2008, he stepped down to youth team manager, a position he kept until the club dissolved amongst financial difficulties.

Photo: Edwin.11

DAVIES, Wyn

*Appearances: 16 Goals: 4 (1972-1973)
Career: Wrexham, Bolton W, Newcastle
United, Manchester C, Manchester
United, Blackpool, Crystal P, Stockport
C, Crewe A. (1960-1977).* Known
affectionately as 'Wyn the Leap' because
of his ball winning skills in the air, came
to Old Trafford for £25,000. He fell out of
favour after only three months when
Tommy Docherty replaced Frank
O'Farrell in the manager's hot seat. He
stayed at the club until the end of the
season before leaving for Blackpool.
Became a baker for Warburton's in
Bolton after hanging up his boots and
now lives in the town in retirement.

DAVIS, Jimmy

*Appearances:1 Goals: 0 (1999-2003)
Career: Manchester United, Swindon
Town, Watford (1999-2003).* A highly
promising winger, joined United as a
trainee in July 1999. Two years later he
made his only first team appearance in a
League Cup tie against Arsenal on 5th
November 2001. He made the bench
for the Champions League but never got
on. Shortly after joining Watford on a
season's loan, he was tragically killed in
a car crash on the M40 on 3rd August
2003. His funeral was held at Redditch
Crematorium, with the United team in
attendance.

DAWSON, Alex

*Appearances: 80 Goals: 45 (1956-1962)
Career: Manchester United, Preston
North End, Bury, Brighton & Hove
Albion, Brentford (1957-1971).* Was the
last player to score a hat trick in a FA
Cup semi-final when United beat
Fulham at Highbury in 1958, having
been a member of the FA Youth Cup
winning sides of 1956 and 1957, the
year the League Championship made
its way to Old Trafford, helped by him
scoring in the last three games of the
season. He became a regular after the

Munich air crash and was a regular until
the arrival of David Herd in the summer
of 1961. Lives in Rothwell,
Northamptonshire, and spent many
years working at Kettering Plastics
factory.

DELANEY, Jimmy

*Appearances: 183 Goals: 28 (1946-
1951) Career: Manchester United (1946-
1951).* Some observers had believed
that he was a suspect purchase when
United bought him from Celtic for
£4,500 in 1946. However, he proved
them all wrong by speeding down the
flank in a red shirt for five full years,
winning a FA Cup winner's medal and a
League Championship title. He only
missed a handful of games before
returning north of the border to join
Aberdeen and remarkably played on
until the age of 43, despite repeated leg
injuries. After retiring, he moved back
to his native Cleland in Scotland where
he worked as a general labourer before
landing a job working in the Ravenscraig
Steel Works. He died from cancer in
September 1989.

DEMPSEY, Mark

*Appearances: 2 Goals: 0 (1985-1986)
Career: Manchester United, Swindon
Town, Sheffield United, Chesterfield,
Rotherham United, Macclesfield (1982-
1991).* A local lad who came up through
the ranks at Old Trafford. Only played
two games for the club, his only league
appearance coming against Ipswich
Town in December 1985. Only a few
months later he was sold to Sheffield
United in a £20,000 deal. After spells at
Chesterfield, Rotherham and
Macclesfield, he worked for United as
head coach to age groups Under-13s
and Under-16s. Dempsey left Old
Trafford in 2009 to coach Tromso in
Norway. Is also involved in youth
projects in North Norway.

DEWAR, Neil

Appearances: 36 Goals: 14 (1933)
Career: *Manchester United, Sheffield Wednesday (1933-1937).* Signed from Scottish outfit Third Lanark for £4,000, with Arsenal, Portsmouth and Newcastle United on his trail. He struggled to make an impact despite scoring 14 goals in 36 games, and went to Hillsborough in exchange for Jack Bell. He started his working life as a trawler fisherman but after finishing his career with Third Lanark, he returned to his home village of Lochilphead where he worked in the countryside. A well-known public speaker during his playing career, he died in January 1982.

DIGBY, Fraser

Appearances: 0 Goals: 0 (1985-1986 & 1992) Career: *Manchester United, Oldham A, Swindon T, Manchester United, Crystal P, Huddersfield T, QPR, Kidderminster H (1985-2003).* Joined United as an apprentice but didn't make a first team appearance before leaving for Swindon Town. He came back to Old Trafford on loan in 1992 as cover for Peter Schmeichel and had to warm the bench, again without making it onto the pitch. Still lives in the Swindon area and he was commercial manager and goalkeeping coach at the County Ground. Is now business development manager for Sports Solutions GB Ltd.

DOCHERTY, John

Appearances: 26 Goals: 7 (1952-1958)
Career: *Manchester United, Leicester City (1952-1958).* Had trials at nine clubs before arriving at Old Trafford, he scored twice against Chelsea in his third game but he was troubled by knee injury during his career. He served in the RAF during his national service and returned to United in 1955-1956 to help win a League Championship with four goals in 16 games. The knee problems continued and his chances became fewer, and he was eventually sold to Leicester City for £6,500.

He returned to Manchester after hanging up his boots, where he worked in the motor trade, later in the insurance and finance industries.Acted as a players' agent before becoming Burnley's chief scout in the early 1980s. He lived in Hale before he died of lung cancer in November 2007, aged 72. A former chairman of the Association of Former Manchester United Players.

DONAGHY, Mal

Appearances: 89 Goals: 0 (1988-1992)
Career: *Luton Town, Manchester United, Luton Town, Chelsea (1978-1994).* A United fan since his childhood in Belfast, Mal achieved his dream move when he joined the Reds from Luton Town for £650,000 in 1988. He started off in central defence alongside Steve Bruce but then moved to full back after the signing of Gary Pallister. He proved his worth by providing experience and a calm head for the emerging youngsters around him. Moved back south after four years to join Chelsea for £150,000 in 1992. Later returned to his native Northern Ireland where he has worked for the Irish FA in a number of development roles since 2000.

DONALD, Ian

Appearances: 6 Goals: 0 (1972-1973)
Career: *Manchester United (1969-1973).* Made his senior debut for the club against Portsmouth in October 1970. When Tommy Docherty took over as manager he was allowed to return to Scotland to join Partick Thistle. In 1980, Donald was appointed to the board of directors at Aberdeen before rising to the position of vice-chairman, and then becoming chairman in 1994. Remained on the board until 2004, when he was appointed as the club's honorary president. His dad was a past chairman and had appointed Alex Ferguson as the Don's boss. He is the chairman and managing director of J F Donald (Aberdeen Cinemas) and is a director of other family companies.

Photo: Leslie Millman

DOWNIE, Alex

Appearances: 191 Goals: 14 (1902-1910) Career: Bristol City, Swindon Town, Manchester United, Oldham Athletic, Crewe Alexandra (1900-1912).
A hard working half back who was a regular in the United team until being dislodged by Dick Duckworth. Despite this, he proved to be a capable deputy for any of the three half back positions. He played ten games in the 1908 title winning season then in 1909, when the FA Cup was won for the first time, he played more games than Alec Berry but didn't feature in the final. In the end, he left for Oldham Athletic for £600 after having been granted a benefit. A qualified engineer, he was on the Munitions Board during the Great War and then ran his open metal brokery business. He died in Withington, Manchester, in December 1953, aged 77.

Dion Dublin
Photo: NPower

DOWNIE, John

Appearances: 115 Goals: 36 (1948-1953) Career: Bradford Park Avenue, Manchester United, Luton Town, Hull City, Mansfield Town, Darlington.
Another scorer of important goals, John was snapped up from Bradford Park Avenue for a club record £18,000 in 1949 as a direct replacement for Johnny Morris. Once he had played a major part in the winning of the 1951-1952 League title by scoring 11 goals in 33 matches, after missing out narrowly in 1949 and 1951. He moved to Luton Town in a £10,000 deal. Worked as a newsagent in Bradford and now lives in Tynemouth in the North East.

DUBLIN, Dion

Appearances: 17 Goals: 3 (1992-1994) Career: Norwich City, Cambridge United, Barnet, Manchester United, Coventry City, Aston Villa, Millwall, Leicester City (1988-2008). Sir Alex Ferguson beat off competition from Chelsea and Everton to clinch Dublin's £1 million signature after losing out to Blackburn Rovers for Alan Shearer. Unfortunately, he broke his leg in a reckless challenge from Crystal Palace's Eric Young and by the time he returned six months later, United had signed Eric Cantona. He failed to make the ten appearances needed for a League winner's medal but was given special dispensation by the Premier League. He struggled to hold down a regular place and was sold to Coventry City after only two seasons at Old Trafford. Dublin has worked as a football television pundit for Sky Sports since his retirement. He has also co-commentated on Premiership and UEFA Champions League matches for Sky, as well as co-presenting 606 on BBC Radio 5 Live. In 2009, he invented a unique percussion instrument that he called "The Dube".

DUCKWORTH, Dick

Appearances: 251 Goals: 11 (1903-1915) Career: Manchester United (1903-1915). One of United's greatest pre-Great War players, was spotted after scoring twice against United's reserves, switched to the half back line and went on to win two League Championships and a FA Cup. Part of the famous Duckworth, Charles Roberts and Alec Bell half back line. A serious knee injury ended his career in 1913 but he stayed on the club's books for another two seasons. He ran a series of pubs in Manchester, Bury, Royton, Castleton, Edenfield and Bacup. He lost his FA Cup winner's medal in his pub in Edenfield but it was found 20 years later in some rubble at the back of the pub and returned to him.

DUNNE, Pat

Appearances: 66 Goals: 0 (1964-1966) Career: Everton, Manchester United, Plymouth Argyle (1960-1970). A goalkeeper who moved to Old Trafford for £10,500 when at the back of queue of six at Goodison Park. Ironically he made his league debut against his former club in place of Dave Gaskell. Unbeaten in his first 15 games, Dunne was on the winning side 13 times, he won a League Championship in 1965 but was never considered to be first choice and lost his place to Harry Gregg. He moved to Plymouth for £5,000 in 1966. Has worked as a psychiatric nurse and a goalkeeping coach in his native Dublin.

DUNNE, Tony

Appearances: 414 Goals: 2 (1960-1973) Career: Manchester United, Bolton Wanderers (1960-1978). From the moment Tony Dunne first pulled on a United shirt in 1964, he was determined not to relinquish it easily. For the next twelve years, his consistency and lightning pace ensured that the left back berth was virtually his own.

Tony Dunne
Photo: Sporting Memorabilia

More than 400 solid performances more than repaid the £5,000 invested in bringing him across the water from Shelbourne. Regular trips home were guaranteed when he was selected by the Republic of Ireland for 32 appearances. During his stay, he amassed a wealth of silverware including a FA Cup winner's medal in 1963, a couple of league championship medals in 1965 and 1967, a European Cup winner's medal in 1968 and the trophy for being voted Ireland's Footballer of the Year in 1969. Even at the ripe old age of 32, when his United career drew to a close, he still managed to play another 166 league games for Bolton Wanderers. Tony finally retired at the age of 37 to concentrate on running a golf driving range in Timperley. A Republic of Ireland full back who earned 32 full caps. Played over 400 League games for the Reds before moving to Bolton in 1973. Now runs a golf driving range in Altrincham, which he opened upon leaving the game. Lives in nearby Sale.

DUNPHY, Eamon

Appearances: 0 Goals: 0 (1962-1965)
Career: *Manchester United, York City, Millwall, Charlton Athletic, Reading (1962-1976).* A promising young player who left Dublin to join United but he never made the grade, was allowed to leave for York City and later made an impact at Millwall. Back in Dublin working as a writer and broadcaster. He is the author of the classic soccer book "Only A Game" and also wrote the international best seller "Unforgettable Fire", the story of U2.

DUXBURY, Mike

Appearances: 299 Goals: 6 (1980-1990)
Career: *Manchester United, Blackburn Rovers, Bradford City (1976-1992).* Born in Accrington and nurtured through the youth system, Mike signed professional terms in 1976 but had to wait a further four years before making his first team debut. His adaptability proved useful to successive managers but it was at right back that he really made his mark. A string of impressive performances resulted in being called up to the England team for whom he made ten appearances in the 1980s. A knee injury hindered his later years and ultimately he joined Blackburn Rovers in 1990. Finished his career at Bradford City where he worked under fellow old boy, Frank Stapleton. Duxbury has been a PE teacher at Bolton School, since 1996 after a spell abroad helping out at soccer schools.

EAGLES, Chris

Appearances: 17 Goals: 1 (2003-2008)
Career: *Manchester United, Watford, Sheffield Wednesday, Watford, Burnley (2003-2010).* Originally came through the youth system at Watford but moved to United academy aged 14, with Danny Webber moving in the other direction, as well as compensation. He made his first team debut at Leeds in October 2003 in a League Cup tie and had a number of spells out on loan before being sold to Burnley in July 2008 for an undisclosed fee.

Eammon Dunphy
Photo: Betfair Poster

EBANKS-BLAKE, Sylvan

Appearances: 2 Goals: 1 (2002-2006)
Career: *Manchester United, Plymouth Argyle, Wolves (2002-2010)*. A product of his home town club Cambridge, he declined terms when United came calling. After signing professional terms, he made his first team debut in a League Cup tie against Crewe with his first goal coming against Barnet a year later. Following a loan spell at Royal Antwerp, he was surprisingly allowed to leave for Plymouth Argyle. Is still in the Premier League with Wolves.

ECKERSLEY, Adam

Appearances: 1 Goals: 0 (2002-2008)
Career: *Manchester United, Barnsley, Port Vale (2004-2008)*. After joining United as a nine year old, he progressed to being a trainee in 2002, signing a professional contract two years later. His only first team appearance came in a Carling Cup win over Barnet in October 2005, the year he was part of the United reserve team that won a clean sweep on trophies. Despite loan spells at home and abroad, he failed to make any further team appearances and was released to join Port Vale. After his release from Vale Park, he moved to Denmark to play for Horsens before signing for AGF on a free transfer in 2010.

ECKERSLEY, Richard

Appearances: 4 Goals: 0 (2007-2009)
Career: *Manchester United, Burnley, Plymouth Argyle (2007-2010)*. The Salford born full back made his debut for United's Under-17 team as a 14 year old. He was a reserve team regular and made his first team and then league debut in January 2009. Later that same season, he won a League Cup winner's medal but in July 2009, he signed a four year deal at Burnley after rejecting a new deal at Old Trafford.

Photo: David Mullen

EDWARDS, Duncan

Appearances: 175 Goals: 21 (1952-1958) Career: *Manchester United (1952-1957)*. One of the finest players to have ever graced the lush Old Trafford turf. Although only 21 when cruelly taken by the Munich air crash, he had already established his magnificent reputation at both club and international level. Potentially one of the best players that the world may have ever seen, he had already won three FA Youth Cup winner's medals, two League Championship medals, FA Cup runners-up medal and two charity shield trophies. He joined United in June 1952 and made his debut just eight months later. He was a genius in the making. Edwards was killed in the Munich air disaster, dying in his sleep at 1.16 am on 21st February 1958. He was the eighth victim. Two stained glass windows are dedicated in his memory at St Francis Church in his home town of Dudley.

Photo: David Mullen

EDWARDS, Paul

Appearances: 68 Goals: 1 (1969-1973)
Career: *Manchester United, Oldham Athletic, Stockport County (1965-1980)*. Joined United from school and in his debut season for the club. appeared in both FA Cup and League Cup semi-finals. He never really established himself in the first team at Old Trafford despite his early promise,and faded from the scene. Still lives in Manchester and works in the parts department of a motor company.

FAGAN, Chris

Appearances: 0 Goals: 0 (2005-2008)
Career: *Manchester United, Lincoln City (2005-2010)*. Hailing from Dublin, he joined United for Home Farm spending three years at the club, playing in the 2007 FA Youth Cup Final defeat at the hands of Liverpool, before being released and joining Hamilton. Signed for Lincoln City from the Glenn Hoddle Academy in June 2009.

FANGZHUO, Dong

Appearances: 3 Goals: 0 (2004-2008)
Career: *Manchester United (2004-08)*. He became the first Chinese player to ever sign for United in January 2004 in a deal worth an initial £500,000 from Dalian Shide. But work permit problems meant that he had to spend two and a half seasons on loan at United's Belgian feeder club Royal Antwerp. After finally being granted a work permit in December 2006, he was a regular for the reserves making his first team debut at Chelsea in May 2007. Couldn't hold down a regular first team place and returned to Dalian Shide after his contract was cancelled by mutual consent in August 2008. Is now playing for Portimonesse in Portugal on the recommendation from Cristiano Ronaldo after a season in Poland with Legia Warsaw.

FEEHAN, Sonny

Appearances: 14 Goals: 0 (1949-1950)
Career: *Manchester United, Northampton T, Brentford (1944-1959)*. The first Irishman to play in goal for United after the Second World War when he was signed from Bohemians in November 1948. He spent 12 months in the reserves before taking Jack Crompton's place in the team but the £11,000 arrival of Reg Allen meant he was surplus to requirements and was sold to Northampton Town for £525 in 1950. Worked as a car salesman before arriving at Old Trafford. He died in March 1995, aged 68.

FERGUSON, Darren

Appearances: 30 Goals: 0 (1990-1994)
Career: *Manchester United, Wolves, Wrexham, Peterborough United (1990-2008)*. The son of Sir Alex, he came through the ranks at Old Trafford and made half his appearances at the start of the 1992-1993 season as a stand-in for the injured Bryan Robson, but he didn't play enough games to qualify for a Championship medal. He spent two more seasons largely in the reserves before being sold to Wolves for £250,000. Went to Peterborough United as player manager in January 2007 until November 2009, when he left by mutual consent. Has been manager of Preston North End since January 2010.

FERRIER, Ron

Appearances: 19 Goals: 4 (1935-1938)
Career: *Grimsby Town, Manchester United, Oldham Athletic, Lincoln City (1933-1947)*. Joined United just after his 21st birthday. He helped United win the Second Division Championship in his first season playing seven games but was unable to hold down a regular first team place and featured more in the reserves, eventually being sold to Oldham Athletic. Became a school teacher and lived in Cleethorpes until his death in October 1991, aged 77.

FIDLER, Frank

Appearances: 0 Goals: 0 (1941-1945)
Career: *Manchester United, Wrexham, Leeds United, Bournemouth, Yeovil Town, Hereford United (1941-1957).* A player who was tipped for a big future at the club until the outbreak of World War Two forced him into serving with the Irish Guards. As a result, he only one made one appearance during the war, a 3-3 draw with New Brighton aged 17, before leaving the club at the end of the conflict to try his luck with Cheshire League Witton Albion. Left at the end of the conflict. Worked at Westlands in Yeovil, then the Post Office then settled in Farnborough in retirement.

FITZPATRICK, John

Appearances: 117 Goals: 8 (1964-1973)
Career: *Manchester United (1964-1973).* Long-haired Scotsman's career was brought to a premature end by knee problems at the age of 25, following a tackle by Leeds' Johnny Giles. By then, he had succeeded Shay Brennan as United's first choice right back after arriving at the club, where he won an FA Youth Cup winner's medal in 1964 as a wing half. He was United's first ever substitute used in a 5-1 defeat against Tottenham. He then returned home to Aberdeen where he eventually set up his own wine importing business.

FLETCHER, Peter

Appearances: 7 Goals: 0 (1970-1973)
Career: *Manchester United, Hull City, Stockport County, Huddersfield Town (1970-1982).* A highly promising striker who left Old Trafford in a £30,000 deal which brought Stuart Pearson from Humberside. He was the highest scorer in the Geneva Youth Tournament and showed early potential, but was then sold as his career appeared to be getting off the ground. Is back living in his native Manchester where he works as a security guard.

FOGGON, Alan

Appearances: 3 Goals: 0 (1976-1977)
Career: *Newcastle United, Cardiff City, Middlesbrough, Manchester United, Sunderland, Southend United, Hartlepool (1967-1977).* A winger whose 45 goals in 105 games for Middlesbrough prompted a £40,000 move to United in 1976 after Tommy Docherty had flown 7,000 miles to watch him play. But after only a matter of months at Old Trafford and without ever starting a game, he was on the move again to Sunderland for a fee of only £25,000. At the end of his career, he settled in Jarrow and worked as a security manager for a north eastern company before taking over the Simonside Arms in South Shields.

Photo: Gustavo Bravo

FORLÁN, Diego

Appearances: 98 Goals: 17 (2002-2004)
Career: *Manchester United (2002-2004).* A goal scorer, signed from Argentinian side, Independiente, in January 2002 in a £6.9 million deal. But for his first 27 games, he couldn't find the back of the net. He became a Fans' Favourite at Old Trafford after scoring a brace in a 2-1 victory at Liverpool. Given his scoring record, it was no surprise when he left for Spanish outfit Villarreal in July 2004 for an undisclosed fee. During his time with United, Forlán won a Premier League, FA Cup and Charity Shield winner's medal. He has been a fixture in the Atletico Madrid front line since his transfer in June 2007.

FORSYTH, Alex

Appearances: 119 Goals: 5 (1972-1978)
Career: *Manchester United (1972-1978).*
Full back with a strong tackle and
inclination to roam forward to show off
his powerful shot, became Tommy
Docherty's second purchase when he
was bought for £100,000 from Patrick
Thistle, where he had previously won a
Scottish League cup medal. He was
released by Arsenal earlier in his career
but became a firm favourite with the
crowd during the Second Division
Championship winning season. He was
also part of the 1976 FA Cup Final losing
side, lost his place to Jimmy Nicholl and
returned to Scotland with Rangers
before finishing up with Motherwell and
Hamilton. Is now the manager of the
Auld Hoose bar in Hamilton, Scotland.

FORTUNE, Quinton

*Appearances: 126 Goals: 11 (1999-
2006)* Career: *Manchester United,
Bolton Wanderers, Doncaster Rovers
(1999-2010).* A teenage star in the
making when he was at Tottenham but
arrived at Old Trafford via Atletico
Madrid, initially as cover on the left hand
side for Ryan Giggs. But Sir Alex
Ferguson soon discovered that he could
play central midfield or left back where
he made most of his first team
appearances. He won the FA Charity
Shield in 2003 and the Intercontential
Cup in 1999 before leaving the club on
a free transfer. Has been without a club
since January 2010 when he left
Doncaster following an injury ravaged
spell.

FOULKES, Bill

Appearances: 682 Goals: 9 (1952-1970)
Career: *Manchester United (1952-1970).*
An all round sportsman who excelled at
rugby (his grandfather had been an
England Rugby League international)
and represented his home county,
Cheshire as a golfer.

Bill Foulkes
Photo: Sporting Memorabilia

However it is as an uncompromising
defender that he will be long
remembered. Born in St. Helens, Billy
signed professional terms at Old
Trafford in 1951 to start a playing career
with the club that was to last for almost
two decades. His record is one of
extremes. At 22 he was selected to play
for England although still only a part-
time player because he had retained his
job working in the mines. Then fourteen
years later he was still going strong at
the age of 36 and was a member of the
1968 European Cup winning side.
Although he never managed to add to
his one full international cap, life was not
without incident. A survivor of the
horror of Munich, he broke the club's
appearance record, won four
championship medals and was part of
the team that won the FA Cup in 1962-
1963. After retiring, he stayed on at Old
Trafford for five years as a youth coach,
then set off working with two clubs in
America, four in Norway and then
Mazda of Japan. He was forced to sell
his collection of medals in 1992 for
£37,000. He was coaching for the
Manchester FA after returning home and
gave tours of Old Trafford to Japanese
tourists because he could speak the
language after his time coaching in the
country.

FOX, David

Appearances: 0 Goals: 0 (2000-2006)
Career: Manchester United,
Shrewsbury Town, Blackpool,
Colchester United, Norwich City (2000-
2010). Born in Stoke-on-Trent, where
his father Peter played in goal, he
signed a professional contract on his
17th birthday in December 2000. After
spending six seasons at Old Trafford
without breaking into the first team, he
was allowed to join Blackpool on a free
transfer. Signed for Norwich City from
Colchester in June 2010.

Photo: Austin Knight, Comedian.

FRY, Barry

Appearances: 0 Goals: 0 (1960-1964)
Career: Manchester United, Bolton W,
Luton T, Leyton O (1962-1968). Joined
Manchester United as an apprentice
winger in April 1960 after turning down
Arsenal, Chelsea and West Ham. An
England schoolboy international, he was
tipped for a big figure. He progressed
through the youth team captained by
Nobby Stiles. Sir Matt Busby awarded
him a two year contract and he was
playing for the reserves at 17, he soon
became friends with George Best but
preferred gambling to football, and
despite being a reserve for the first
team twice, he was allowed to leave on
a free transfer. Has become one of the
most colourful managers in the modern
game, helped Barnet into the Football
League, has managed Southend,
Birmingham and Peterborough U where
he is now director of football.

GALBRAITH, Danny

Career: Manchester United (2006-
2009). Signed by United on his 16th
birthday after spending three years as a
schoolboy at Hearts. He played in the
2007 FA Youth Cup final defeat to
Liverpool scoring in the penalty shoot
out. He was released in 2009 returning
to Scotland to join Hibs.

GARTON, Billy

Appearances: 51 Goals: 0 (1984-1990)
Career: Manchester United,
Birmingham City (1984-1990). Came
through the ranks with the likes of Mark
Hughes and Norman Whiteside, he was
a useful back-up utility defender but he
was troubled by a number of injuries.
He made his debut in a League Cup tie
against Burnley in 1984 and his last
appearance came against Coventry
City four years later before he was
forced to retire at the age of 25 after
starting to suffer blinding headaches. In
2000, Garton and his family relocated to
San Diego where he runs the Carmel
Valley Manchester youth soccer club.

GASKELL, Dave

Appearances: Goals: (1956-1967)
Career: Manchester United, Wigan
Athletic, Wrexham (1956-1972). When
he made his United debut in the 1956
Charity Shield aged only 16 years and
19 days, he was and still is the youngest
player to play for United. But he still
had to wait 12 months for his league
debut against Spurs. He played
regularly as cover for Harry Gregg and
was in goal for the 1963 FA Cup Final
victory over Leicester. The arrival of Pat
Dunne relegated him to third choice.
When they both left, Alex Stepney and
Jimmy Rimmer joined, so he decided to
move on. After retiring, he coached in
South Africa before taking a job in
Kuwait. He returned to the UK to live in
Wrexham where he worked as a
salesman for a concrete making firm,
then became regional manager of a
flooring company. He is now retired.

Photo: Sporting Memorabilia

GIBSON, Colin

Appearances: 79 Goals: 9 (1985-1990)
Career: *Aston Villa, Manchester United, Port Vale, Leicester City, Blackpool, Walsall (1978-1994).* Joined from Aston Villa for £275,000 in 1985 during the reign of Ron Atkinson, he made a good name for himself for three seasons as a hardworking utility player but a serious knee ligament problem suffered in a pre-season game in Sweden stopped his career in its tracks. A series of operations and comebacks resulted in further breakdowns and eventually led to a £100,000 move to Leicester in 1990. A former England B international who became a football agent and worked for Radio Leicester before moving to Radio Derby as a senior sports reporter.

GIBSON, Don

Appearances: 108 Goals: 0 (1950-1955)
Career: *Manchester United, Sheffield Wednesday, Leyton Orient (1950-1961).* Another local lad who made it through from the youth system to secure a first team place. Enjoyed eight years as a professional winning a League Championship winner's medal with the club before losing his place in a re-shuffle switch, which resulted in Tommy McNulty switching to right full back and

Johnny Carey switching into the half back line and he moved to Sheffield Wednesday for £8,000 in June 1955. He ran a confectionery shop in Burnage near Manchester that he had bought in 1951. He sold sweets and signed autographs until retiring to Blackpool.

GIBSON, Terry

Appearances: 27 Goals: 1 (1985-1987)
Career: *Tottenham Hotspur, Coventry City, Manchester United, Wimbledon, Swindon Town, Barnet (1979-1995).* He joined United for around £600,000 in a deal which took Alan Brazil to Highfield Road. But he never quite lived up to expectations especially as he found first team chances hard to come by under both Ron Atkinson and Sir Alex Ferguson, even though sometimes the club found scoring goals on a regular basis difficult. Terry has coached at Barnet and Fulham as well as running a company which sold bikes in club colours. Is now based in southern Spain, works for Sky on their coverage of Spanish football. Also helps coaching Northern Ireland and scouted for Man City and Bolton.

GIDMAN, John

Appearances: 95 Goals: 4 (1981-1986)
Career: *Aston Villa, Everton, Manchester United, Manchester City, Stoke City, Darlington (1972-1989).* Joined United in 1981 in the same deal that took Mickey Thomas and £50,000 to Everton to become Ron Atkinson's first signing for the club. He soon became a favourite of the Stretford End but a number of injuries dented the impact that he made at the club. He was a FA Cup winner in 1985. He played almost 100 league matches before joining Man City in 1986 after becoming surplus to requirements. Former Kings Lynn manager, has been living in Marbella on the Costa del Sol since the mid-1990s.

Johnny Giles plaque unveiling
Photo: The Labour Party

GILES, Johnny

Appearances: 115 Goals: 13 (1959-1963) Career: Manchester United, Leeds United, West Bromwich Albion (1959-1976). United had snapped Irishman Giles him up from Home Farm as a 17 year old for a £10 signing on fee. However, he broke a leg at the start of his Old Trafford career but recovered well enough to impress at inside forward and outside right. He won an FA Cup winner's medal in 1963 and after being dropped, following the Charity Shield defeat at Everton, he decided to ask for a transfer rather than wait for his next chance in the first team and joined Leeds United for £35,000. Later played for West Brom before moving into management. Former player manager of the Republic of Ireland and twice managed WBA, turned his hand to journalism with the Daily Express and is now a leading football analyst on Irish radio station NewsTalk. Also works for RTE television. Is the brother-in-law of Nobby Stiles.

GILL, Tony

Appearances: 14 Goals: 2 (1986-1990) Career: Manchester United (1986-1990). A short career was blighted by injuries. He made his debut at Southampton in January 1987 but then spent two nearly two years on the sidelines with an Achilles tendon injury. Then just as it looked as if he had established himself in the first team, an accidental clash with Nottingham Forest's Brian Law saw him suffer a broken leg and shattered ankle. He never played professionally again. He became a youth team coach at Bristol Rovers and then assistant manager at Bath before quitting the game completely. He is now believed to be living in the Hull area.

GILLESPIE, Keith

Appearances: 14 Goals: 2 (1993-1995) Career: Manchester United, Wigan Athletic, Newcastle United, Blackburn Rovers, Leicester City, Sheffield United, Charlton Athletic, Bradford City (1993-2009). A member of the same United youth team as the likes of David Beckham, Robbie Savage, Paul Scholes, Ryan Giggs and Gary Neville, he scored his first United goal against Bury in the FA Cup, but he was never able to displace Andrei Kanchelskis on the right wing. He was valued at £1 million in the £7 million deal which took Andrew Cole from Newcastle to Old Trafford in January 1995. He returned to Northern Ireland for the 2009-2010 season where he played for Glentoran. But is now without a club.

GIVENS, Dons

Appearances: 9 Goals: 1 (1969-1970)
Career: Manchester U, Luton T, QPR,
Birmingham C, Bournemouth, Sheffield
United (1969-1980). He won his first
international cap before making his
United debut and played almost as
many games for the Republic of Ireland
as he did United by the time of his
£15,000 move to Luton in April 1970. He
coached Arsenal's youth team and then
worked in Switzerland before becoming
the Republic's Under-21 boss a decade
ago. Has also had two spells as
caretaker manager of the senior team.

GOATER, Shaun

Career: Manchester United, Rotherham,
Notts Co, Bristol C, Manchester C,
Reading, Coventry C, Southend U
(1989-2006). Was spotted by United
scouts but was unable to break into the
first team squad. He moved to
Rotherham where he started to make his
name in English football. Has now
returned home to Bermuda where he is
the business development officer for East
End Asphalt.

GODDARD, Karl

Career: Manchester United, Bradford
City, Exeter City, Colchester United,
Hereford United (1986-1992). A Leeds
born defender who was a junior at
United but left without being offered
professional terms. He lives in his native
city and works as a builder.

GOODWIN, Fred

Appearances: 107 Goals: 8 (1953-1960)
Career: Manchester United, Leeds
United, Scunthorpe United (1953-1966).
A dual sportsman, in the summer he
played cricket for Lancashire. He won
League Championship medals in 1956
and 1957 but wasn't a regular before
Munich because of the likes of Duncan
Edwards and Eddie Coleman. He was
lucky enough to have stayed in England
for that fateful trip in February 1958 and
then helped the club reach the FA Cup
Final in the same season. He moved to
Leeds United in 1960 in a £10,000 deal.
He went into management firstly with
Scunthorpe but emigrated to the US
where he managed Minnesota Kicks.
He continued to live in the city and ran a
successful travel business.

Don Givens, (front row 4th from left) *Photo: (c) JOHN BARRINGTON / nineteen21*

GORAM, Andy

Appearances: 2 Goals: 0 (2001)
Career: Oldham Athletic, Notts County,
Sheffield United, Manchester United,
Coventry City, Oldham Athletic (1981-
2002). Goram had achieved legendary
status with Rangers by the time he
joined United on loan from Motherwell
for the title run-in during the 2000-2001
season when Fabien Barthez and
Raimond van der Gouw were ruled out
of action. He played two games after
United were reported to have paid
around £100,000 to secure his services.
The former Scotland international
cricketer lives in Rutherglen, Glasgow,
where he runs a pub and has worked as
a goalkeeping coach. He also does
some after dinner speaking and attends
functions for Rangers fans.

GOWLING, Alan

Appearances: 71 Goals: 18 (1967-1972)
Career: Manchester U, Huddersfield T,
Newcastle U, Bolton W, Preston NE
(1967-1982). Gowling turned down a
place at Cambridge University to
continue his football career at Old
Trafford. He was likely to have achieved
had he not been competing for a place
in the front line with the likes of Best,
Law and Charlton. A regular goal
scorer for the reserves, he scored on his
league debut against Stoke but it wasn't
until 1970-1971 that he became a first
team regular. He scored four goals in a
game against Southampton but despite
being converted into a midfielder, he
was sold to Huddersfield Town for
£60,000. Is the general manager of a
chemicals company in Buxton and has
been a pundit for BBC Manchester.

George Graham & Terry Venables *Photo: Commander Idham*

GRAHAM, Arthur

Appearances: 37 Goals: 5 (1983-1985)
Career: Leeds U, Manchester United,
Bradford C (1977-1986). Graham was
fast approaching the veteran stage of his
career when Ron Atkinson paid £45,000
to lure him from Elland Road, but he did
a superb job as a stop gap on United's
left wing after Steve Coppell had been
forced out the game through injury. He
provided ammunition for Frank Stapleton
but he lost his place, once Jesper Olsen
was signed in 1984. Coached children
with the Eddie Gray coaching schools,
now based in Wetherby and runs his
own schools called First Touch Soccer.
Also coaches at Leeds' Academy.

GRAHAM, Deinoil

Appearances: 4 Goals: 1 (1987-1990)
Career: Manchester United, Barnsley,
Preston NE Carlisle United, Stockport
County, Scunthorpe United, Halifax
Town (1987-1996). Named after his
mother's favourite Welsh Village, he only
had limited first team chances despite
an impressive scoring record in United's
junior sides. His only goal came in an
FA Cup tie at QPR, he suffered a broken
arm not long afterwards and was sold at
the start of the 1991-1992 season to
Barnsley for £50,000. Is now a football
development officer in Conway, Wales.

GRAHAM, George

Appearances: 46 Goals: 2 (1972-1975)
Career: Aston Villa, Chelsea, Arsenal,
Manchester United, Portsmouth, Crystal
Palace (1962-1977). He was Tommy
Docherty's first signing for United, re-
uniting a partnership that started at
Chelsea, the manager claiming that his
£120,000 new boy was as good as
German superstar Gunter Netzer.
Along with several other new faces,
Graham helped saved the club from
relegation in his first season, he was
captain for the second season despite
having a large majority of the crowd on
his back. He was soon dropped and
swapped for Ron Davies.

Coached various clubs before taking
charge of Millwall, moved on to Arsenal
with great success before accepting an
unsolicited gift and was sacked. Has
since managed Leeds and Spurs but is
now a media pundit.

GRAY, David

Appearances: 1 Goals: 0 (2005-2010)
Career: Manchester United, Crewe A
Plymouth A, Preston NE (2005-2010).
He came through the ranks of Hearts in
Scotland before securing a £50,000
move to Old Trafford on his 16th
birthday. Broke into United's reserves
within 12 months and his debut came in
the League Cup against Crewe, in
September 2006. Was released on a
free transfer at the end of the 2009,
joining Preston on a two year deal.

GRAY, Michael

Appearances: 0 Goals: 0 (1988-1990)
Career: Sunderland, Blackburn R, Leeds
United, Wolves, Sheffield W (1992-
2010). A Sunderland born left back who
was on schoolboy forms for United for
two years. He was offered a contract by
the club but decided against signing it
and instead became an apprentice at his
home town club, going onto win three
caps for England. He retired in June
2010 and has worked for the BBC
writing a blog for the website, and as a
summariser on Five Live.

GREAVES, Ian

Appearances: 75 Goals: 0 (1953-1960)
Career: Manchester United, Lincoln C,
Oldham A (1953-1962). A Busby Babe,
he replaced Bill Foulkes at right back for
the closing stages of the 1955-1956
season and helped the club clinch the
League title. He was also a member of
the 1958 FA Cup losing side but a knee
injury ended his Old Trafford career. He
went into coaching before managing
Bolton, Oxford and Mansfield. He
scouted for both United before retiring.
He sadly died after a long illness in
January 2009 in Ainsworth, Bury aged 76.

GREEN, Brad

Appearances: 0 Goals: 0
Caught the eye of United scouts in
Tasmania and spent a month at Old
Trafford as a 15 year old. He wasn't
offered a contract by United but was by
Walsall following a successful trial, but
opted to finish his schooling in Australia.
Is now playing in the Australian Football
League (Aussie Rules) for Melbourne
Demons.

GREENHOFF, Brian

*Appearances: 271 Goals: 17 (1973-
1979) Career: Manchester United,
Leeds United, Rochdale (1973-1983).*
Although Brian was the younger of the
two Greenhoff's to play for United, he
actually signed the dotted line six years
before his brother, Jimmy, joined the
club. Originally a full back, he played
most of his career as a central defender.
He made his debut in an all action
midfield alongside Sammy McIlroy in an
unsuccessful fight against relegation,
but he helped the club bounce back
and to win the Second Division title at
the first attempt. A FA Cup winner
against Liverpool in 1977, he was sold
by Dave Sexton to Leeds United in 1979
for a fee of £350,000 after a string of
injuries interrupted his career. After
retiring, he lived in Rochdale and
worked as a sales representative for a
sports goods wholesalers, William
Lindop Sports. Now retired and living in
Spain.

Photo: criminalrobot

GREENHOFF, Jimmy

*Appearances: 123 Goals: 36 (1976-
1981) Career: Leeds United,
Birmingham City, Stoke City,
Manchester United, Crewe Alexandra,
Port Vale, Rochdale (1963-1983).* Older
brother of Brian, Jimmy joined United in
November 1976. He had already proved
himself to be a classy striker with
Leeds, Birmingham and seven years at
Stoke City when he was signed for a
bargain fee of £120,000. He linked up
well with Stuart Pearson and scored in
the 1977 FA Cup Final and in the same
season, he became the first United
player to score a hat trick in almost
three years. Two years later, he was on
the losing side when United lost another
Cup Final to Arsenal. He was hit by
injuries towards the end of his career
and departed Old Trafford for Crewe.
Ran his own insurance business,
Greenhoff Peutz & Co in Audley, on the
outskirts of Stoke ,until almost losing
everything 14 years ago. Ended up
working nights in a Stoke
pharmaceutical company and does
some corporate hosting at Old Trafford.

GREENING, Jonathan

*Appearances: 27 Goals: 0 (1998-2002)
Career: York City, Manchester United,
Middlesbrough, WBA, Fulham (1996-
2010).* Signed for an initial £500,000 in
March 1998, a month after spending a
successful four days on trial at Old
Trafford. He was an unused sub in the
Champions League Final win over
Bayern Munich in 1999 but couldn't hold
down a regular place in the first.
Frustrated by the lack of first team
chances, he followed United's assistant
manager, Steve McClaren, to
Middlesbrough along with team mate
Mark Wilson. In July 2010, he signed a
permanent deal at Fulham following a
successful loan spell in West London.

A collection of badges from the 1970's featuring both Greenhoff brothers Jimmy (top left and middle of second row) and Brian (just below the Championship trophy to the right)

Photo: Leslie Millman

GREGG MBE, Harry

Appearances: 247 Goals: 0 (1957-1967)
Career: *Doncaster Rovers, Manchester United, Stoke City (1952-1966).* Irish international who followed in Reginald Allen's footsteps to become the country's most expensive goalie when he put his signature to the transfer forms bringing him to Old Trafford from Doncaster Rovers for £23,000 in 1957. Originally hailing from Derry, Harry earned rave reviews for his international performances at the 1958 World Cup finals in Sweden and earned a total of 24 full caps. 1958 proved to be an eventful year. In addition to the World Cup, he played in the FA Cup final against Bolton Wanderers, was one of the fortunate survivors of the Munich air crash and was widely praised for his efforts in helping his colleagues escape from the wreckage. He spent a decade at the club before leaving for Stoke City. He later managed Shrewsbury Town, Swansea City, Crewe Alexandra and Carlisle United, and was also on United's coaching staff before returning to Northern Ireland, where he ran the Windsor hotel in Port Stewart for many years until his retirement. Gregg was awarded the MBE in 1995 and was made an Honorary Graduate of the University of Ulster in 2008.

GREGORY, Tony

Appearances: 0 Goals: 0
Career: A Bolton born junior goalkeeper at United in the early 1964-1965 but never made the grade, wasn't offered a contract, dropping out of the game completely. As Tony St.Clair and Tony Sinclair, he found fame after following his family and taking up wrestling a year after leaving Old Trafford in 1966, winning a string of titles. He became a referee later in his career but retired after suffering a stroke in Hanover, Germany, where he is a longtime resident, near Hannover.

GRIFFITHS, Clive

Appearances: 7 Goals: 0 (1973-1976)
Career: *Manchester United, Plymouth Argyle, Tranmere Rovers (1973-1976).* He lost his United place after making seven first team appearances. His debut came against Burnley in October 1973. But with relegation looming, he was dumped into the reserves remaining on United's books until 1976 when he left for America and was signed by Chicago Sting, coached by former United defender Bill Foulkes. Stayed on in the States and coached youth teams for the US Soccer Federation. He now lives in Kansas City and has recovered from cancer for a second time, travels the world promoting his company, The International Soccer Program.

GRIFFITHS, Jack

Appearances: 176 Goals: 1 (1933-1940)
Career: *Wolverhampton Wanderers, Bolton Wanderers, Manchester United (1929-1940).* The move to United breathed new life into his career, he became an international trialist in 1936 the same season as helping the club to the Second Division title, missing only one game. The full back's career was ended with the outbreak of World War Two. After retiring, he worked as a masseur in Hyde, Cheshire.

GRIMES, Ashley

Appearances: 107 Goals: 11 (1977-1983) Career: *Manchester United, Coventry City, Luton Town, Stoke City (1977-1991).* He had already had an unsuccessful trial at United as a 15 year old when five years later, Tommy Docherty paid £20,000 to land him from Bohemians. But during his six years at Old Trafford, his development wasn't helped by injury and illness, and he was eventually sold to Coventry City in August 1983 for £200,000. Coached at Stoke and Huddersfield, now lives in Lostock, Bolton.

GRIMSHAW, Tony

Appearances: 2 Goals: 0 (1974-1979)
Career: *Manchester United (1974-1979).*
Joined United as an associate schoolboy
in 1972 before signing apprentice forms
in April 1974. He signed professional
forms in December, the same year. His
debut came against Brentford in the
second round of the League Cup in
September 1975. A month later he
made his only league appearance as a
sub in a win over Leeds United at Elland
Road. But a broken leg against Aston
Villa in a Central Lane game kept him
out of action for two seasons and ended
any hopes of a professional career. Is
now a policeman with the Greater
Manchester Police.

HALL, Jack

Appearances: 73 Goals: 0 (1932-1936)
Career: *Manchester United, Tottenham
Hotspur (1932-1940).* He spent the first
12 months of his United career in the
reserves until Charlie Hillam conceded
10 goals in three games. Then he got
his first team chance in the 1933-1934
season when the club narrowly avoided
the drop into the Division Three. He had
established himself as the club's
number one by the time the club won
the Second Division Championship, but
then surprisingly opted to remain in the
second tier with Spurs than stay at Old
Trafford. He was an electrician by trade
and was employed by the Manchester
Electrical Company.

HALSE, Harold

*Appearances: 124 Goals: 50 (1908-
1912) Career: Clapton Orient, Southend
United, Manchester United, Aston Villa,
Chelsea, Charlton Athletic (1905-1923).*
Started repaying his £350 transfer fee
when he opened his goal scoring
account in the first time of his United
career. A top opportunist marksman of
his day, he won League Championship
and FA Cup winner's medals, he

became the first player to appear in
three Cup Finals with different clubs, he
also netted six times in the 1911 Charity
Shield win over Swindon Town. He was
sold to Aston Villa for £1,200. Scouted
for Charlton for a couple of years before
opening a tobacconist's shop in Walton
on Naze. Died in Colchester County
Hospital in March 1943, aged 63.

HANLON, Jimmy

Appearances: 70 Goals: 22 (1938-1949)
Career: *Manchester United, Bury (1938-
1950).* Was promoted to the first team
after scoring 10 goals in 7 games for the
reserves after rejecting a move to
Accrington Stanley. His contribution
helped United climb away from the foot
of the First Division table, finishing as
leading scorer in 1938-1939 with 12
goals in 27 games. In the first season
after the war, he was part of the United
set up that finished runners up but then
failed to hold down a regular place. He
continued to live in his native
Manchester until his death in January
2002.

HARDISTY, Bob

Appearances: 0 Goals: 0 (1958-1959)
Career: *Darlington, Manchester United
(1946-1959).* Noted for being one of
England's greatest ever amateur
internationals, playing in three Olympic
Games for Great Britain. He enjoyed a
long association with Sir Matt Busby who
named him captain of the 1948 Olympic
team. In the wake of the Munich air
crash, even though he was retired,
Busby famously told assistant Jimmy
Murphy "Send for Hardisty" to help him
run and play for the reserves. He was
one of three players from the great
Bishop Auckland amateur team to play
for United during their darkest ever
time. A teacher and a football coach, he
has a street named after him in County
Durham. He died in Durham in October
1986, aged 64.

The Duncan Edwards Room at Dudley Museum *Photo: Black Country Museums*

HARROP, Bobby

Appearances:11 Goals: 0 (1957-1959)
Career: *Manchester United, Tranmere
Rovers (1957-1961).* An England youth
international who joined United from
school. Signed professional terms in
May 1954 but he had to wait until the
wake of the Munich air crash for his first
team debut. He was pressed into action
for the FA Cup sixth round replay
against WBA in March 1958, but after
that had to play second fiddle to Stan
Crowther. He left Old Trafford for
Tranmere Rovers in November 1959 in a
joint £4,000 deal involving Gordon
Clayton. Lived in Broadstairs, Kent, and
worked as a carpet layer, then a
drayman with Bass Charrington, before
becoming a ranger at North Foreland
Golf Club and was working on the day
he died in November 2007, aged 71.
He was also a respected local referee
and managed the reserve teams of
several Kent clubs.

HAWKSWORTH, Tony

Appearances: 1 Goals: 0 (1955-1958.)
Career: *Manchester United. (1955-
1958).* The Sheffield born goalkeeper is
one of a small handful of players to have
won three successive FA Youth Cup
winner's medals in 1954, 1955 and 1956.
He had only played three reserve
games for United when he was called
into the first team for a game against
Blackpool in October 1956 after an
injury to Ray Wood. Hawksworth was
doing his national service at the time
and needed special permission to leave
the army barracks in Catterick, North
Yorkshire, to play in the game. It turned
out to be his only first team appearance.
He was posted to Germany at the time
of the Munich air crash and visited his
former youth team mate, Duncan
Edwards, on the night he died. In
December 1958, he was allowed to
leave United and signed for non-league
Bedford Town.

After playing non-league football, he
worked for a sweet company before
joining British Gas until his retirement in
1995. He now lives in Dronfield
Woodhouse in Derbyshire.

HAYDOCK, Frank

Appearances: 6 Goals: 0 (1960-1963)
Career: *Blackpool, Manchester United,
Charlton Athletic, Portsmouth, Southend
United (1956-1970).* After spending
three years working as an engineering
apprentice he turned professional in
1960. Highly rated by Matt Busby who
had several chances to sell him, despite
Haydock only being a fringe player all
offers were rejected. In 1963, Charlton
Athletic were successful with a £10,000
bid and he played the rest of his career
in the south for Athletic, Portsmouth and
Southend.. Is now retired after spending
many years working as an hotelier in
Blackpool.

HAYES, Vince

*Appearances: 128 Goals: 2 (1901-1905
& 1908-1911) Career: Newton Heath,
Brentford, Manchester United, Bradford
City, Rochdale (1901-1914).* A
boilermaker by trade, was signed as a
centre half but then became a left half.
His career took a setback with two
broken legs and he spent a year out of
the game before making a comeback
with Brentford. Rejoined United the
following season in London, playing in
the 1909 FA Cup success. Lost his place
in the side the following season and
moved to Bradford City. Vince coached
the Norwegian Olympic team for the
Stockholm games, he then coached
Austrian side Weiner SV, returned home
to work for the Players' Union before
becoming player manager of Rochdale
until 1919, was then secretary-manager
of Preston and managed Madrid. He
ended his working life running a pub in
Stockport and then a hotel in Prestwich.

HEALY, David

Appearances: 2 Goals: 0 (1999-2000)
Career: *Manchester United, Port Vale, Preston, Norwich City, Leeds United, Fulham, Sunderland, Ipswich Town (1999-2010).* A Northern Ireland international, came to Old Trafford just before his 20th birthday in August 1999. He made his first team debut in a League Cup tie at Aston Villa two months later. After making his first team debut as a sub against Ipswich the following season, chances were limited and in December 2000, he moved to Preston for £1.5 million. Is currently on loan to Ipswich Town from Sunderland.

HEATON, Tom

Appearances: 0 Goals: 0 (2005-2010)
Career: *Manchester United, Swindon Town, Cardiff City, QPR, Rochdale, Wycombe Wanderers, Cardiff City (2005-2010).* The England Under-21 international played for the United Under-17s before signing as a trainee in July 2002. The next season, he picked up a FA Youth Cup winner's medal. A reserve team regular, he was sent out on loan to gain first team experience but he couldn't break into the first team and was released at the end of the 2009-10 season, signing for Cardiff in July 2010.

HEINZE, Gabriel

Appearances:83 Goals: 4 (2004-2007)
Career: *Manchester United (2004-2007).* Signed by United for £6.9 million in July 2004 from PSG, and immediately established himself as first choice left back becoming popular with fans. He was voted Sir Matt Busby Player of the Year in his first season at Old Trafford. He won a Premier League winner's medal in 2006-2007 but lost his place to Patrice Evra following injury. Liverpool had a £8 million bid rejected before he became the third United star after David Beckham and Ruud van Nistelrooy, to sign for Real Madrid in August 2007 for

Gabriel Heinze
Photo: Articularnos

£8 million. In July 2009, he moved back to France to join Marseille for an undisclosed fee.

HERD, David

Appearances: 263 Goals:144 (1961-1968) Career: *Stockport C, Arsenal, Manchester U, Stoke C (1950-1969),* Started his career at Stockport County alongside his father, Alex. He joined United in a £35,000 deal from Arsenal in 1961. The goals flowed after the arrival of Denis Law, he scored twice in the 1963 FA Cup Final and won League Championship winner's medals in 1965 and 1967. He even had the distinction of putting three goals past three different keepers in one match against Sunderland. Herd bowed out of the game as a player at Stoke after a broken leg all but ended his United career. Spent 18 months as manager of Lincoln City before being replaced by a young Graham Taylor. He bought a garage in Urmston which he ran for many years.

HERON, Tommy

Appearances: 3 Goals: 0 (1957-1961)
Career: *Manchester United, York City (1958-1966).* Was first spotted by United scouts playing for Portadown in Northern Ireland. An outside left, he made his debut against Preston North End in March 1958 shortly after the Munich air crash, wearing the number 11 shirt which was Dave Pegg's before his death. He switched to full back but found that his first team chances were limited and he signed for York City in May 1961. Lives in retirement in Manchester after working for his former United team mate, Alan Wardle, as a driver for his stationery business.

HIGGINBOTOM, Danny

Appearances: 7 Goals: 0 (1996-2000)
Career: *Manchester United, Derby County, Southampton, Stoke City, Sunderland, Stoke City (1997-2010).* A Manchester born defender, joined the club as a trainee and made his League debut against Barnsley in May 1998. Was sent out on loan but still found his chances were few and far between, ending up with a £2 million transfer to Derby County in July 2000. He joined Stoke City for a second time in July 2008 in a £2.5 million deal after a spell at Sunderland, and remains at the Britannia Stadium. The battling full back has also played for Derby County and Southampton.

HIGGINS, Mark

Appearances: 8 Goals: 0 (1985-1986)
Career: *Everton, Manchester United, Bury, Stoke City (1976-1990).* His father, John Higgins, was part of the Bolton Wanderers team that beat United in the 1958 FA Cup Final. He had retired after a successful career with Everton but came out of retirement to join United in a £60,000 deal in December 1985 but he didn't last long, only playing a handful of games before Sir Alex Ferguson took over and sold him to Bury for a cut price £10,000. He became director of sales at Buxton Spa Bakeries in Derbyshire but is still a regular visitor to Goodison Park.

HILL, Andy

Appearances: 0 Goals: 0 (1983-1984)
Career: *Manchester United, Bury, Manchester City, Port Vale (1983-1998).* A member of the United team which finished runners up to Watford in the 1982 FA Youth Cup, signed professional forms with the club but was allowed to make the short move to Bury without ever playing first team game. After retirement, Hill became Head of Youth Development at Bury before joining American side Nevada Wonders as Academy director. He now runs his own football academy named "Pro-Vision North West" which operates in the Greater Manchester area.

Star Badges circa 1956-8 *Photo: Leslie Millman*

Photo: Gordon Hill

HILL, Gordon

Appearances: 133 Goals: 51 (1975-1978) Career: Millwall, Manchester United, Derby County, Queens Park Rangers (1972-1980). Millwall were the first club to give Gordon a crack at League football. He impressed sufficiently to persuade Tommy Docherty to shell out £70,000. Almost immediately, he was called up by England for the first of six caps. Played over 100 games in three eventful years on the left wing at Old Trafford, he formed a formidable wing combination with Steve Coppell then followed The Doc to Derby for £250,000 in 1978, despite his outstanding record of 17 goals in 36 games in Dave Sexton's first season in charge. England international winger, is now the owner and head coach of United FC, in McKinney, Texas. Used to live in Tampa, Florida, where he worked as a tennis and football coach.

HOGG, Graeme

Appearances: 83 Goals: 1 (1984-1988)
Career: *Manchester United, WBA, Portsmouth, Notts County, Brentford (1984-1998).* Former Scotland Under-21 international whose 6ft 1in frame slotted comfortably into the back four, keeping out the likes of Gordon McQueen and Kevin Moran. He was unlucky to miss the 1985 FA Cup Final victory over Everton through injury even though he had been a regular fixture in the side. After Paul McGrath and Kevin Moran started to emerge on the scene, he found his chances few and far between and was allowed to leave for the South Coast after eight years at Old Trafford when Portsmouth offered £150,000 for his services in 1988. Later played for Hearts, Notts County and Brentford before finally retiring from the game in 1998. Is now back living in his native Scotland and works as a television engineer.

HOGG, Steven

Appearances: 0 Goals: 0 (2004-2005)
Career: *Manchester United, Shrewsbury Town, York City (2005-2009).* Joined United as a trainee after growing up in Bury but was released after only a season at the club. He has dropped out of the game after leaving York City in 2009.

HOLLAND, Reg

Appearances: 0 Goals: 0 (1957-1960)
Career: *Manchester United, Wrexham, Chester City (1957-1966).* Twice a FA Youth Cup winner during his time at Old Trafford, he went on to captain the reserves and sat on the first team bench three times without ever seeing any action. Was sold to Wrexham in March 1960 for £2,000. Joined the Staffordshire Police force and was on the beat for 27 years until his retirement in 1994.

Munich Tribute outside Old Trafford *Photo: James Maskell*

HOLTON, Jim

Appearances: 63 Goals: 5 (1972-1976)
Career: *West Bromwich Albion,*
Shrewsbury Town, Manchester United,
Sunderland, Coventry City, Sheffield
Wednesday (1968-1981). Scottish
international 'Big Jim' was sent off twice
in his first nine games for United
following his arrival from Shrewsbury
Town in an £80,000 deal. He did much
to help the club avoid relegation in his
first season at Old Trafford only for the
trap door to open beneath them 12
months later. He rose to colt hero status
and was voted Player of the Year and
then had to endure two broken legs
during his stay, the first coming midway
through the Second Division promotion
campaign, a second in his comeback
for the reserves forcing his departure in
1976. Ran the Old Stag pub in Coventry
until his sudden death in 1993.

HOMER, Tom

Appearances: 25 Goals: 14 (1909-1912)
Career: *Aston Villa, Manchester United*
(1904-1912). Wrote himself into club
history for being the first United player
to score at Old Trafford in a defeat to
Liverpool in February 1910. A centre
forward, only spent three years at the
club and found chances limited with
Knocker West preferred, despite his
very good games to goals ratio. A knee
injury forced his early retirement. He
became a licensee in his native
Birmingham.

HOUSTON, Stewart

Appearances: 250 Goals: 16 (1973-
1980) Career: Chelsea, Brentford,
Manchester United, Sheffield United,
Colchester United (1967-1985). A
Scotsman with one full international cap
to his name, was lured south to play for
Chelsea and Brentford before Tommy
Docherty paid the Bees a bargain
£55,000 in 1973 to help shore up a then
leaky defence.

Stewart gave reliable service at left
back for over six years, he won a
Second Division Champion medal in
1975 and then a FA Cup final loser's
medal 12 months later. He missed out
against Liverpool in 1977 with torn
ankle ligaments and was never the
same again, even though he spent
another three years at the club. Has
twice been caretaker manager of
Arsenal and taken control of QPR,
coached a number of other clubs and is
now scouting for The Gunners.

HOWARD, Mark

Appearances: 0 Goals: 0 (2004-2006)
Career: *Manchester United (2004-*
2006). Went to the same Salford school
as United team mate Phil Bardsley, he
spent two years at Old Trafford in the
juniors and reserves without making a
first team appearance, and was released
at the end of the 2005-2006 season. He
was, however, offered a deal by former
Manchester United reserve team coach,
Rene Meulensteen, who had taken over
at Brondby where he was voted Player
of the Year in 2007. In December 2009,
he joined another Danish club, AGF, on a
three year contract.

Photo: *www.leaguemanagers.com*

Photo: Nigel Wilson

HOWARD, Tim

Appearances: 77 Goals: 0 (2003-2007) Career: Manchester United, Everton (2003-2010). An American international who arrived at the club from the New Metrostars in a $4 million deal in 2003 to replace Fabien Barthez. He became the first American to win a FA Cup winner's medal in his first season. His second season wasn't as smooth, sharing the goalkeeping duties with Roy Carroll. He was then replaced as first choice by Edwin van der Sar and left the club permanently in March 2007 to join Everton, following a loan spell at Goodison Park.

HUCKER, Peter

Appearances: 0 Goals: 0 (1988) Career: Queens Park Rangers, Cambridge United, Oxford United, West Bromwich Albion, Manchester United, Millwall, Aldershot, AFC Bournemouth (1980-1991).

Joined United on loan in 1988 from Oxford United but never played a first team game, before returning to his parent club. Gave up a milk round franchise to open successful soccer schools in East London and Essex. Also coaches the keepers at Spurs Academy and at Millwall. Has also worked as a sports coach for local councils.

HUGHES, Mark

Appearances: 467 Goals: 163 (1983-1986 & 1988-1995) Career: Manchester United, Barcelona, Bayern Munich, Chelsea, Southampton, Everton, Blackburn Rovers (1980-2002). Making a popular return from Barcelona for £1.5 million in 1988, Hughes quickly picked up from where he had left off three years earlier. Not only was he a regular goal scorer, his physical presence supplied much needed aggression and strength to the front line. By the time that he brought his second spell at Old Trafford to an end, leaving for Chelsea in 1995 in a £1.6 million deal, he had won two Premier League titles, three FA Cups, a League Cup, two Charity Shields, a Cup Winners Cup and a UEFA Super Cup. Since retirement, Hughes has entered the management circle, firstly in charge of the Wales international team, before stints as boss of Blackburn and Manchester City.

Photo: Kate Boydell

HUGHES, Phil

Appearances: Goals: (1981-1983)
Career: *Manchester United, Leeds
United, Wigan Athletic, Bury, Rochdale,
Scarborough.(1981-1991).* A member
of United's 1982 FA Youth Cup Final
team, he started both legs in the Final
against Watford but wasn't offered a
professional contract by the time. After
serving as an apprentice for two
seasons, he joined Leeds United on a
free transfer. Worked as a policeman
before becoming a goalkeeping coach
after his career was ended early, has
been employed by Leeds, Grimsby and
Burnley before linking up with his
current employers, Bolton Wanderers.

HUGHES, Phil

Appearances: 0 Goals: 0 (1981-1983)
Career: *Manchester United, Bury,
Wigan Athletic, Rochdale, Scarborough
(1983-1992).* Phil spent two years at Old
Trafford as an apprentice and was a
member of their 1982 FA Youth Cup
runners up side, only to leave at the end
of the following season without putting
pen to paper on a professional contract.
After his career was ended early
through injury, he joined the police for a
short spell before returning to football
as goalkeeping coach at Leeds,
Grimsby, Burnley and since January
2010, Bolton Wanderers.

HUNTER, Geoff

Appearances: 0 Goals: 0 (1976-1979)
Career: *Manchester United, Crewe
Alexandra, Port Vale, Wrexham (1976-
1991).* Signed for United as an
apprentice and impressed enough in
the youth ranks to be offered a
professional contract in November 1976.
Despite being a regular in the Central
League team, he never managed to
make the break through into the first
team squad and was released on a free
transfer to join Crewe. After leaving
Wrexham, he returned to his home town
Hull, where he took a job working as a
sales rep.

HUNTER, Reg

Appearances: 1 Goals: 0 (1958-1959)
Career: *Manchester United, Wrexham
(1956-1962).* Initially arrived at the club
on trial from Colwyn Bay, signing
professional forms just after his 18th
birthday. He won a FA Youth Cup
winner's medal in his first season at the
club at the expense of West Ham United.
His only first team appearance came at
Aston Villa in December 1958, as
deputy for Warren Bradley at outside
right in a 2-0 victory. But after failing to
realise his early promise, he left Old
Trafford for Wrexham in February 1960.
Went to work in the Wrexham offices of
Border Breweries.

HUTCHINSON, Tommy

Scottish international who had a fantastic
career playing for a number of clubs
but is probably best remembered for
his time with Blackpool and Coventry
City. in fact, Coventry fans voted him
their most popular player during their
First Division years. He was part of the
United squad which toured Australia
after the 1983-1984 season, making
appearances against Australia,
Nottingham Forest and Juventus. He
played another game for the club in
May 1985 in Peter Foley's testimonial
against Oxford United. He now lives in
South Wales and is a football
development officer for Bristol City.

Denis Irwin (back row 2nd from left)
Photo: Austin Knight, Comedian

INCE, Paul

Appearances: 281 Goals: 29 (1989-1995) Career: *West Ham United, Manchester United, Inter Milan, Liverpool, Middlesbrough, Wolverhampton Wanderers, Swindon Town, Macclesfield Town (1984-2007).* A midfield maestro who joined the fold from West Ham in 1989 in a controversial £2.4 million deal that still rankles with West Ham fans to this day. The 'guvnor's' aggressive style earned him rave reviews and he was very much the driving force behind United winning back-to-back Premier League titles. He also played in two FA Cup Final wins and a Cup Winners Cup victory. Unfortunately it was rumoured that all was not well in the dressing room and he was eventually sold on to Inter Milan for £7 million in 1995, much to the surprise of many supporters. After leaving Swindon Town in 2006, where he was a player coach, he joined Macclesfield Town as player manager before retiring from playing and leaving the club a year later. He has since managed Blackburn Rovers and has had two separate spells in charge of Milton Keynes Dons, his second spell ending in resignation at the end of the 2009-2010 season.

IRVING, Richard

Appearances: 0 Goals: 0 (1989-1995) Career: *Manchester United, Nottingham Forest, Macclesfield Town (1992-1997).* Irving joined United after leaving school and was a member of the FA Youth Cup losing side in 1993. He was offered professional terms but couldn't make the step up into the senior squad, and was sold to Nottingham Forest in 1995 for £75,000. Later also played for Macclesfield Town but gave up his professional footballing career in 1997 and is now a commercial airline pilot. Lives among the footballers in Alderley Edge, Cheshire.

Paul Ince
Photo: ruth1066

IRWIN, Denis

Appearances: 529 Goals: 35 (1990-2002) Career: *Leeds United, Oldham Athletic, Manchester United, Wolverhampton Wanderers (1983-2004).* The success of Dennis Irwin must cause a few blushes at Leeds United. They let him join Oldham Athletic in May 1996 after only 72 league starts at Elland Road. Three years later, he was valued at £650,000 when he moved from Boundary Park to Old Trafford. The years since his move in June 1990 have proved even this to be a bargain price for the acquisition of one of the most consistent performers in the Football League. By the time he left, he did so with seven Premier League titles to his name. Three FA Cups, a League Cup, Cup Winners Cup, Champions League, Super Cup, Intercontinental Cup and three Charity Shields. As a Republic of Ireland international, he represented his country on 56 occasions and scored four goals. Denis has been working as a presenter on MUTV since 2004. He has also done some work for RTE in his native Ireland.

JACKSON, Tommy

Appearances: 23 Goals: 0 (1975-1978)
Career: Everton, Nottingham Forest,
Manchester United (1967-1978). He
was signed by Tommy Docherty on a
free transfer with the view to captaining
the reserves following promotion back
to Division One. But he briefly helped
plug the midfield until Gordon Hill
arrived from Millwall to take his place in
a new formation. He was largely a
reserve afterwards and was given a free
transfer in 1978. Former Northern
Ireland international, lives in
Glengormley and works as a self-
employed upholsterer for Bannon & Co
in Belfast. Also coaches a kids team.

JAMES, Steve

Appearances: 161 Goals: 4 (1968-1975)
Career: Manchester United, York City,
Kidderminster Harriers (1968-1972).
The England youth international who
joined United as an apprentice in July
1965, before signing professional terms
18 months later in December 1966. He
was earmarked as the natural successor
to the legendary Bill Foulkes when he
retired, and for a while he tried to fill his
shoes. He made his debut against
Liverpool in October 1968 but it wasn't
until the return game with the
Merseyside club, two months later, that
he got a long run in the team. The
arrival of Ian Ure saw his chances
limited until Frank O'Farrell took over as
manager and gave him another run. But
when Tommy Docherty was appointed
manager and signed Jim Holton from
Shrewsbury Town, his days at the club
were numbered and former United
boss, Wilf McGuinness, eventually took
him to York City in 1975. ended his
playing days at Kidderminster Harriers
and since leaving football, he has
worked in the licensing trade, most
recently as steward at the Liberal Club
in Cradley.

JEFFREY, David

Appearances: 0 Goals: 0 (1979-1982)
Career: Manchester United (1979-
1982). Hailing from Newtownards,
Northern Ireland, he spent three years
at Old Trafford as a youth team player
before returning home to join Linfield,
after failing to make the breakthrough
into the first team squad. He has been
the manager of Linfield since 1997.

JOHNSEN, Ronny

Appearances: 150 Goals: 9 (1996-2002)
Career: Manchester United, Aston Villa,
Newcastle United (1996-2004). The
Norwegian international who was
capable of playing in defence or
midfield. Ronny was snapped up from
Turkish side Besiktas for £1.5 million in
1996, and helped the club to win four
Premier League titles, an FA Cup and a
Champions League Winner's medal.
After forming a solid partnership with
Jaap Stam, he remained with United until
the end of the 2001-2002 season when
his contract expired, and was given a
free transfer following fellow Norwegian
Oyvind Leonhardsen to Villa Park. He
has played for Norway in the
International Masters Tournaments and
now deals in Real Estate in Tonsberg,
Norway.

JOHNSON, David

Appearances: 0 Goals: 0 (1992-1995)
Career: Manchester United, Bury,
Ipswich Town, Nottingham Forest,
Sheffield Wednesday, Burnley, Sheffield
United (1994-2006). Started off his
career at United as a trainee in 1992 and
after two years, was offered a professional
contract. Twelve months later, he hadn't
made a first team appearance despite
sitting on the bench for a Champions
League clash with Galatasary, and he
joined Bury. He did win a FA Youth Cup
with United. Was forced into an early
retirement with a back problem. Now
works for Umbro in sponsorship.

JOHNSON, Eddie

Appearances: 1 Goals: 0 (2001-2006)
Career: *Manchester United, Coventry City, Crewe A, Bradford C, Chester City (2003-2009).* A product of the Crewe Academy, he joined United in 1999 signing as a trainee two years later. In October 2003, he made his only first team appearance in a League Cup tie at Leeds, and the same season was part of United's FA Youth Cup winning side. He was one of seven players released at the end of the 2005-2006 season, joining Bradford City. He moved to the United States in 2009 to play for Austin Aztex who are managed by former Everton star, Adrian Heath.

Photo: Tuborg Light

JONES, David

Appearances: 4 Goals: 0 (2003-2007)
Career: *Manchester United, Preston, Derby County, Wolves (2003-2010).* First joined United as a 10 year old and captained United to FA Youth Cup success in April 2003. The following season, he made his first team debut as a substitute in a League Cup clash with Arsenal, and made his full debut in the FA Cup against Exeter. In the 2004-2005 season, he was named captain of the reserves and led them to Premier Reserve League glory. He was unable to shift Roy Keane and Paul Scholes from the first team and once Michael Carrick was signed, a bid from Derby County was accepted. The former England Under-21 international joined Wolves in June 2008 for £1.2 million.

JONES, Mark

Appearances: 121 Goals: 1 (1950-1958)
Career: *Manchester United (1950-1958).* A Munich victim, he came up through the ranks after joining United, when he was a bricklayers apprentice, as deputy for Allenby Chilton. He had to wait for his first team chance but he was one of several young players given an extended run in the side in 1954-1955, and he was ever present the next season when the League Championship was secured. He was part of the squad that retained the title but lost out to Jackie Blanchflower in the 1957 FA Cup Final and the half back line of Colman, Jones and Edwards, which was on a par with the famous line up in Edwardian times of Duckworth, Roberts and Bell. He was only 24 when he became one of the victims of the Munich air crash. He is buried in Wombwell near Barnsley.

JONES, Peter

Appearances: 1 Goals: 0 (1954-1960)
Career: *Wolves, Manchester United, Wrexham, Stockport County (1953-1968).* Was an amateur at Old Trafford before leaving for Wolves but returned after a season because of home sickness. Working part-time at Simpsons Steelworks, he signed part-time forms taking a job as a cabinet maker. He made his only first team appearance in place of Roger Byrne as left back in November 1957 in a 3-0 home defeat to Portsmouth. He narrowly avoided being on the plane at Munich, being called up as a replacement for Geoff Bent who recovered from injury in time to travel. He spent two years on national service before being sold to Wrexham after being demobbed. He lives in Swinton, and worked for a chemical company for over 30 years after trying window cleaning, running a Salford fish and chip shop, and working for a textile company in Carrington.

JONES, Peter

Appearances: 1 Goals: 0 (1957-1960) Career: Manchester United, Wolves, Manchester United, Wrexham, Stockport County (1952-1968). A trainee coal miner in Swinton, was on the Old Trafford ground staff before spending a season at Wolves. He rejoined United signing a professional deal in April 1955. A FA Youth Cup winner in 1956, he made his only first team appearance against Portsmouth in October 1957 replacing Roger Byrne. He was due to be part of the ill-fated trip to Belgrade, being called up as cover for Geoff Bent who subsequently recovered and sadly died on the Munich runway. Jones was sold to Wrexham after his national service. He tried his hand at window cleaning and running a fish and chip shop in Salford before joining a Carrington textile company. In 1977, he went to work for a chemical company, staying until his retirement. He still lives in Swinton.

JONES, Richard

Appearances: 5 Goals: 0 (2005-2008) Career: Manchester United, Colchester United, Barnsley, Yeovil Town, Hartlepool United, Oldham Athletic (2005-2010). Jones joined the United Academy at the age of the nine and later skippered United's reserves. He made five first team appearances with his debut in October 2005 coming against Barnet in the League Cup. He remained at Old Trafford until June 2008 after a number of loan spells, before being released and joining Hartlepool. He was given a free transfer at the end of the 2009-2010 season and joined Oldham on a free transfer.

JONES, Tommy

Appearances: 22 Goals: 4 (1934-1935) Career: Tranmere Rovers, Sheffield Wednesday, Manchester United, Watford, Arsenal (1926-1946).

Tommy moved to United in June 1934 and started the season partnering fellow new boy, George Mutch, at inside forward in the opening weeks of the campaign. But he was unable to hold down a regular first team place during his only season at the club and left at the end of the season. After retiring, he worked on the coaching staff of Tranmere, Workington and Birmingham City before joining WBA as physio in 1966. He died shortly after his retirement in August 1971.

JORDAN, Joe

Appearances: 126 Goals: 41 (1977-1981) Career: Leeds United, Manchester United, Southampton, Bristol City (1970-1989). When Joe arrived at Old Trafford from Leeds in a record £350,000 deal in January 1978, he brought with him a fearsome reputation. Although able to regularly find the net, he also was a tigerish competitor, afraid of no-one. This attitude served him well during his three year stay before he left to try his luck in Italy with AC Milan for a fee of £350,000, after he was unable to agree terms for a new deal in the early days of Ron Atkinson's reign at the club. Scottish international striker, has managed Bristol City, Hearts and Stoke City, and has also been assistant manager of Huddersfield and caretaker boss of Portsmouth. Is now at Spurs.

JOVANOVIC, Nikola

Appearances: 26 Goals: 4 (1979-1982) Career: Manchester United (1980-1982). He was United's first foreign signing when Dave Sexton gambled £300,000 to sign him from Red Star Belgrade. He got a run in the team after injuries to Kevin Moran and Martin Buchan in 1980-1981 but struggled to adjust to the pace of English football, and his contract was cancelled in November 1982. Didn't settle at Old Trafford and became general manager of FC Lovcen in 2007.

KANCHELSKIS, Andrei

Appearances: 161 Goals: 36 (1990-1995) Career: *Manchester United, Everton, Manchester City, Southampton (1990-2006).* Kanchelskis may have been of Ukranian descent but everyone understood the language of his feet. He had the power to turn a game with deft control and incredible speed. He was signed for £650,000 in March 1991 and he soon became a regular, despite competition from Mike Phelan and Bryan Robson. He was part of United's first ever League Cup winning side before helping them lift the first of their Premier League crowns. He then helped do the double in 1994 and finished the following season as leading scorer with 15 goals. But a falling out with Sir Alex Ferguson led to his £5.5 million departure to Everton. Continued to play in England for Everton Man City, and Southampton. In 2007, Kanchelskis returned to Russia and was appointed sporting director of FC Nosta Novotroitsk. However in December 2009, he became manager of Torpedo Moscow.

KEANE, Roy

Appearances: 480 Goals: 51 (1993-2005) Career: *Nottingham Forest, Manchester United (1990-2005).* Born in Cork, Roy was launched into English soccer by Nottingham Forest who had the foresight to snap him up from little Irish side, Cobh Ramblers, in 1990. Within three years, he had become a regular international and one of the hottest properties in the League. With a host of top clubs fighting for his signature, United paid £3.75 million and broke the transfer record in July 1993 to add his talents to the midfield. He captained the club from 1997 until his departure in 2005, and by then he had won seven Premier League titles, four FA Cups and a Champions League. Controversy wasn't far around any corner during his career but he will be remembered as one of United's greatest ever players. Won 67 caps for the Republic of Ireland. Since his retirement in 2006, Keane moved into management, having been in charge of Sunderland between 2006 and 2008. He is currently manager of Ipswich Town.

KEELEY, Walter

Appearances: 2 Goals: 0
Career: *Manchester United war time guest.* Served in the RAF during the war, both of his appearances came against Halifax in successive weeks in the 1944-1945 season. He became a plumber and sadly died in March 1995.

Photo: babasu

KELLY, Jimmy

Appearances: 1 Goals: 0 (1975-1976)
Career: *Manchester United (1974-1976).* Came through the ranks and made his only League appearance as a sub against Wolverhampton Wanderers at Old Trafford in December 1975. But it wasn't until he left United and moved across the Atlantic that his career really took off playing under the guidance of Bill Foulkes at the Chicago Sting. He also played for Tulsa Roughnecks, Los Angeles Aztecs,Portland Timbers and was later a team mate of Jimmy Greenhoff in Toronto. Kelly has been the head coach at the College of DuPage in Glen Ellyn, Illinois, since 1987 and has been playing in the NJCAA Division I Men's soccer program since 1990.

Photo: Andy Brannan

KENNEDY, Paddy

Appearances: 1 Goals: 0 (1953-1955)
Career: *Manchester United, Blackburn Rovers, Southampton, Oldham Athletic (1953-1961).* An Irish school boy international from Dublin, he moved to England as a 15 year old. He was the first ever captain to lift the FA Youth Cup when United beat Wolves over two legs, but found his path to the first team blocked by the skipper of the Busby Babes,Roger Byrne. He had been converted from a centre half into a full back after joining United. His only first team appearance came against Wolves in October 1954 when a number of senior players were away on international duty. During his time at his first three League clubs, they all won League titles but he never played enough games for any of them to win a medal. He continued to live in the Urmston area of Manchester working in the Massey Ferguson factory in Trafford Park. A leading figure in local football for many years, he died in Trafford Hospital in March 2007, aged 72, after suffering from ill-health for some time.

KIDD, Brian

Appearances: 264 Goals: 70 (1967-1974) Career: *Manchester United, Arsenal, Manchester City, Everton, Bolton Wanderers (1967-1981).* Kidd went to the same school in Collyhurst as Nobby Stiles and exploded onto the scene at a very young age. He played in the 1967 FA Charity Shield against Tottenham Hotspur and made his League debut the following week against Everton. He won a European Cup Winner's medal on his 19th birthday, scoring in the 4-1 win over Benfica at Wembley, and was selected for England in his early twenties. Appearing to be on the threshold of a brilliant career, Brian suffered an inexplicable loss of form which coincided with United's relegation from the First Division, and he was sold to Arsenal for £110,000. Later played for Manchester City, Everton and Bolton Wanderers. Then managed Barrow, Preston and Blackburn, has been assistant manager at Manchester United, Leeds and England among others, and is now assistant manager at Man City, after running the youth team.

KINSEY, Albert

Appearances: 1 Goals: 1 (1964-1965)
Career: *Manchester United, Wrexham, Crewe Alexandra, Wigan Athletic (1962-1973).* An England schoolboy international hailing from Merseyside, was picked up by United when he left school. After making his way through the junior teams, he was selected for the Central League side. He was a FA Youth Cup winner in 1963-1964 season. His only appearance for the first team came in place of the injured Denis Law for an FA Cup tie against Chester in January 1965, which saw him score in a 2-1 victory. But frustrated by a lack of first team opportunities, he asked for a transfer and moved to Wrexham, managed by former United star Jack Rowley. He emigrated to Australia in 1974 and after he finished playing for local clubs in the Sydney area, he worked for a couple of pharmaceutical companies as a supervisor in the manufacturing process. For over a decade, he has been running his own carpet and flooring retailing business based in Shelly Beach, New South Wales.

KIROVSKI, Jovan

Appearances: 0 Goals: 0 (1992-1996)
Career: *Manchester United, Crystal Palace, Birmingham City (1993-2004).* The first American to sign for the club when he joined in 1992, he was the leading scorer for the reserves in 1996 but work permit regulations prevented him from playing for the first team, and he had to leave at the end of that season for Borussia Dortmund. He returned to the States after leaving St. Andrews and is currently a team mate of David Beckham at LA Galaxy.

KOPEL, Frank

Appearances: 12 Goals: 0 (1967-1969)
Career: *Manchester United, Blackburn Rovers (1966-1972).* Spotted by United chief scout Joe Armstrong, he arrived at Old Trafford from his native Scotland as a 15 year old.

The Scottish school boy international was converted into a full back, he made his debut as a sub against Burnley and a month later in October 1967, he made his first start against Nottingham Forest in place of Tony Dunne. But with chances limited, he was sold to Blackburn Rovers for £25,000 just before his 20th birthday. He had a spell on the coaching staff of Dundee United where he is regarded as a club legend, and he was also assistant manager of both Arbroath and Forfar where his son Scott played. He ran a business before becoming sales manager for a radio station, and now lives in Angus.

LANE, Martin

Appearances: 0 Goals: 0 (1977-1982)
Career: *Manchester United, Chester City, Coventry City, Wrexham, Chester City, Walsall (1979-1992).* A full back born in Altrincham, he joined United as a trainee in 1977 and went on to play at junior and reserve team levels at the club for the next five years. But he left in 1982 without making a first team appearance and joined Chester City. Worked in the security industry.

LARSSON, Henrik

Appearances: 13 Goals: 3 (2007)
Career: *Manchester United (2007).* The legendary striker joined United from Helsingborg during the Swedish close season and scored on his debut against Aston Villa in the FA Cup. He scored his first Premier League goal against Watford and then on his last appearance at Old Trafford against Lille in the Champions League. United were keen to extend the deal but Larsson wanted to keep a promise to his family that he would return to Sweden . United won the Premier League title at the end of the season and were granted special dispensation to award him a medal along with Alan Smith. He played floorball in Sweden but since 2009 he has been the manager of second division Landskrona BoIS.

Photo: Paul-Ipswich

LAW, Denis

Appearances: 404 Goals: 237 (1962-1973) Career: Huddersfield Town, Manchester City, Manchester United, Manchester City (1956-1974). One of the most deadly finishers to grace the game, Law had the ability to produce results whilst also able to entertain the crowd. Earned his nickname 'The King' by scoring 237 goals for the club in 404 games after his record £110,000 transfer from Torino. An FA Cup winner in 1963, he was voted 'European Footballer of the Year' a year later. Law helped United to League Championships in 1965 and 1967 but he missed the European Cup Final win over Benfica with a knee injury. A hugely popular figure with the fans, he was given a free transfer by Tommy Docherty and returned to Maine Road where he relegated United with a back heel at the end of the 1973-1974 season. That was to prove to be his last ever League game. Undoubtedly one of football's great personalities. Since leaving the playing side, has worked as a commentator on both television and radio, and is a popular after dinner speaker. Has since won a battle with prostate cancer. Lives in Bowden, Cheshire.

LAWTON, Nobby

Appearances: 44 Goals: 6 (1958-1963) Career: Manchester United, Preston North End, Brighton, Lincoln City (1958-1972). Joined United as an amateur, training two nights a week whilst working for a coal merchant. He turned professional after the Munich air crash and made steady progress after making his debut against Luton in April 1960. Enjoyed his best run in the team in 1961-1962 including a hat trick against Nottingham Forest on Boxing Day 1961, but when Paddy Crerand arrived at the club, he was allowed to join Preston. He had several jobs before returning to Newton Heath and worked as a sales director at an export packaging company. Sadly lost a battle to cancer in April 2006.

LEA, Michael

Appearances: 0 Goals: 0 (2007-2008) Career: Manchester United, Scunthorpe U, Chester City (2007-2010). Joined United as a trainee and was a regular for the youth team and the reserves, but he couldn't make the break through into the first team squad and was allowed to leave on a free transfer at the end of his contract in June 2008. Has had two spells at Hyde United, one at Rochdale and is now at Colwyn Bay since Chester went out of business.

LEE, Kieran

Appearances: 3 Goals: 1 (2006-2008) Career: Manchester United, QPR, Oldham Athletic (2006-2010). Signed on a youth contract in 2004 and progressed through the youth teams into the reserves whom he captained in 2006-2007. He scored on his first team debut against Crewe in the League Cup but his Premier League debut came against Chelsea in May 2007. He won the Denzil Haroun Reserve Team Player of the Year but after being given a free transfer in the summer of 2008, he joined Oldham.

Photo: Fee (df82)

LEIGHTON, Jim

Appearances: 94 Goals: 0 (1988-1991)
Career: Manchester United, Arsenal,
Reading, Sheffield United (1988-1993).
Followed his former boss Sir Alex
Ferguson from Aberdeen for a British
record £450,000 fee in June 1988. Seen
as one of the best shot stoppers in the
business, he enjoyed a good first season
with the club keeping 14 clean sheets,
but then suffered a lack in confidence
which ended up costing him his place
from the 1990 FA Cup Final replay
against Crystal Palace. From then on,
he had to play second fiddle to Les
Sealey and in February 1992, he
returned to Scotland with Dundee. Now
lives in the Cults area of Aberdeen and
works as a goalkeeping coach for
Huntly in the Highland League and the
Scottish Under-21 team, having
previously worked for his local club. He
also runs the Jim Leighton Goalkeeping
School.

LEWIN, Derek

Appearances: 0 Goals 0 (1958-1959)
Career: Oldham Athletic, Accrington
Stanley, Manchester United (1953-
1959). A talented wing half who scored
in three successive FA Amateur Cup
Finals which were all won by Bishop
Auckland. He was a close friend of
many of the Busby Babes. After being
selected for the 1956 Olympics, he was
told to train at his nearest club which
was United. He was particularly close to
Geoff Bent and after the crash, Jimmy
Murphy asked him to join United (along
with Bob Hardisty and Warren Bradley)
even though it was the club's policy not
to play amateurs in the first team.
Instead, he played for the reserves in
the Central League. He is now a retired
company director who lives outside
Chorley. He combined playing with
working for his bacon importing
business in Manchester.

Our site: www.where-are-they-now.co.uk

LEWIS, Eddie

Appearances: 24 Goals: 11 (1952-1956)
Career: *Manchester United, Preston North End, West Ham United, Leyton Orient (1952-1963).* Scored on his debut for United against WBA in November 1952 and ended the season with 9 goals from 11 games. But the arrival of Tommy Taylor from Barnsley saw his first team chances almost dry up and he was sold to Preston for £10,000, despite his impressive start to his Old Trafford career. Has coached in Burkina Faso, Ghana, Nigeria and South Africa where he has been living and working since 1972. Works as a pundit for the Super Sport channel and PA Sports, he was also a technical advisor to Moroka Swallows in 2007.

LIEVESLEY, Leslie

Appearances: 2 Goals: 0 (1931-1932)
Career: *Doncaster Rovers, Manchester United, Chesterfield, Torquay United, Crystal Palace (1929-1940).* Joined United from Doncaster where he was leading scorer with 12 goals in 14 games in his first season but was a wing half-back, and he made his debut against Charlton Athletic in March 1932. He made his only other appearance against Oldham a week later, before returning to the reserves where he stayed for his second and final season before moving to Chesterfield. He went into coaching after the Second World War in Holland and Spain before joining Turin in 1947, but a promising coaching career was ended in a plane crash at Superga, just to the West of Turin in May 1949. He died, aged 38.

LINKSON, Oscar

Appearances: 59 Goals: 0 (1908-1913)
Career: *Manchester United (1908-1913).* A full back who was spotted on a continental tour while he was playing for an amateur side the Pirates, he was never considered to be a first team regular until his last two seasons with the

club. He was still allowed to leave to play for Shelbourne in Ireland. One of the United players to lose his life in the Great War, he was killed in action in France in August 1916, while serving in the Footballers Battalion. He encountered the wrath of the authorities before going to the Western Front by absenting himself to play for QPR. He was initially reported missing and no trace of his body has ever been found.

LIVINGSTONE, George

Appearances: 46 Goals: 4 (1908-1914)
Career: *Sunderland, Liverpool, Manchester City, Manchester United (1900-1914).* Played for both United and City, and Rangers and Celtic in Scotland, was banned as part of the illegal payments scandal in 1906, was signed by United three years later and scored twice against City on his debut. He missed out on the 1909 FA Cup Final but played 10 games when they secured the League title a year later, and went on to become player coach for the reserves before the Great War. After the war, he managed Dumbarton and Clydebank before having lengthy spells as trainer at Rangers and Bradford. He retired to Dumbartonshire in 1935 and he lived there until his death, aged 74, in 1950.

LOWEY, John

Appearances: 0 Goals: 0 (1974-1977)
Career: *Manchester United, Blackburn Rovers, Sheffield Wednesday, Blackburn Rovers, Wigan Athletic, Chesterfield, York City, Preston North End, Chester City (1974-1988).* He spent three seasons at Old Trafford, two as a professional, but never made the breakthrough into the first team squad. He was allowed to join Chicago Sting on a free transfer. Finished his career in Australia, lives in Brisbane where he has business interests that include a Beauty Therapy training school and a licensed securities company.

LYNCH, Mark

Appearances: 1 Goals: 0 (2001-2004)
Career: *Manchester United, Sunderland, Hull City, Yeovil Town, Rotherham United, Stockport County (2001-2010).*
A locally born full back, he was unlucky enough to score an own goal on his only first team appearance in the Champions League against Spanish side, Deportivo La Coruna. In July 2004, he was given a free transfer and joined Sunderland but only lasted one season at the Stadium of Light. After dropping through the divisions, he signed for Stockport County in July 2010.

Photo: *United Nights*

MACARI, Lou

Appearances: 401 Goals: 97 (1973-1984) Career: *Manchester United, Swindon Town (1966-1985).* Although he was born in Edinburgh, Luigi Macari's family hail from the same region of Italy as Sophia Loren. Joined United for £200,000 in 1973, a record fee for a Scottish player at the time, shortly after Tommy Docherty took over at Old Trafford. Initially used in the front line, it was only when Tommy Docherty switched him to midfield that he made his most telling contribution. He suffered relegation and then promotion in his first two seasons, he played in three FA Cup Finals and a League Cup Final during his 11 years service before accepting the role of player manager at Swindon in 1984. Scottish international striker, has managed Swindon Town, West Ham, Stoke City (twice), Birmingham, Celtic, Huddersfield. Lives in Stoke-on-Trent, works as a pundit on MUTV and for a local paper. Also owns the Lou Macari Chip Shop near Old Trafford.

MACDOUGALL, Ted

Appearances: 18 Goals: 5 (1972-1973)
Career: *Liverpool, York City, Bournemouth, Manchester United, West Ham United, Norwich City, Southampton, Bournemouth, Blackpool (1966-1980).* Frank O'Farrell paid £200,000, a record fee for a third division player, in September 1972, in a bid to turn around his side's flagging fortunes. But he had only been at Old Trafford for five months when he was transfer listed by Tommy Docherty after he failed to settle in the North. Ironically, five years after he left the club, United were paid to pay Bournemouth an extra £22,000 as part of a goal-related clause in his complicated transfer. Became the owner of sports shops in Bournemouth and a licensee of a public house near Romsey, Hampshire. Emigrated to Vancouver, Canada, with his French Canadian wife, where he has become a wealthy property developer. Returned to England for a spell as Portsmouth's reserve team coach, then moved to the USA where he worked with San Jose Earthquakes and the United States Air Force Academy. Now lives in Atlanta, USA, and was Director of Youth with the Atlanta Silverbacks before setting up his own club, Atlanta Spurs, with former Notts County pro, Paul Smith.

MACKEN, Jon

Appearances: 0 Goals: 0 (1995-1996)
Career: *Manchester United, Preston NE, Manchester City, Crystal P, Ipswich T, Derby C, Barnsley, Walsall (1996-2010).* A forward from Blackley, Manchester. Was snapped up by United as a youngster and joined the club after leaving school in 1995. Twelve months later, he signed pro terms but left in July 1997 for Preston in a £250,000 deal. The Republic of Ireland international signed a deal in August 2010 to join Walsall until the end of the 2010-2011 season.

MADDLETHWAITE, Bert

Appearances: 0 Goals: 0 (1947-1951)
Career: *Manchester United, Blackpool (1947-1953).* Spent three years on the United ground staff and did enough to be offered a professional terms for the last year of his stay at Old Trafford, and was allowed to leave for Blackpool without making a first team appearance. But his stay at the seaside was blighted by injuries. After playing for non-league clubs Stalybridge Celtic and Glossop North End, he went into the licensing trade and worked in a number of pubs across the North. He retired in Sheffield where he died in March 2007, aged 74.

MAIORANA, Giuliano

Appearances: 7 Goals: 0 (1989-1994)
Career: *Manchester United (1989-1994).* A left winger who was working in a bakery when he signed for Histon. Spotted by a United scout who invited him for a trial. Persuaded Sir Alex Ferguson to give him a four year deal and pay £30,000. This saved Histon who were £23,000 in debt. Debuted as a sub against Millwall in January 1989 but suffered a serious knee injury after just a handful of games and never played for the club again. He then returned home to work in his family's upholstery business. Has since played in United's Masters Football Team.

MANLEY, Thomas

Appearances: 195 Goals: 41 (1931-1939) Career: *Manchester United, Brentford (1931-1952).* The scorer of one of the two vital goals against Millwall which preserved United's Division Two status in May 1934. Two years later he scored 14 goals in 31 appearances, including four in a game against Port Vale as they secured the Second Division Championship. Despite leaving the club for Brentford in the last season before the Second War World, he came back to guest during the War, Manley went back to London in peace time and continued to play until he was 39. He then returned home to Cheshire and took over the running of the Avenue Inn in Comberbach.

MARSH, Phil

Appearances:1 Goals: 0 (2003-2007)
Career: *Manchester United, Blackpool (2006-2008).* Marsh made his only first team appearance against Crewe in the League Cup. He was released in June 2007 and joined Blackpool. After playing for a number of non-league clubs including FC United, he is now at Stalybridge Celtic.

MARTIN, Lee

Appearances: 109 Goals: 2 (1987-1994)
Career: *Manchester United, Bristol Rovers, Huddersfield Town (1988-1998).* Hit the headlines when he scored the only goal to win the 1990 FA Cup at the expense of Crystal Palace. It was only one of two goals that he scored for the club. His big break came when Arthur Albiston left the club and he appeared to have secured a regular place in the starting line up until Clayton Blackmore emerged. In 1991 he collected a Super Cup winner's medal and even though he struggled to hold down a regular first team place, he regularly captained the reserves . In January 1994, he left Old Trafford for Celtic. Is now working in West Cheshire helping young people find qualifications, courses or jobs.

United Nights. To find out more visit: *www.unitednights.co.uk*

MARTIN, Lee

Appearances:3 Goals: 0 (2005-2009)
Career: *Manchester United, Stoke City, Plymouth A, Sheffield U, Nottingham F, Ipswich T, Charlton A (2005-2010).* A product of the Wimbledon youth ranks, he was wanted by a number of big clubs including Liverpool, Arsenal and Spurs. Eventually United paid an initial £200,000 for him in December 2003, and he quickly established himself in the reserves. He made his first team debut against Barnet in the League Cup in October 2005. After failing to break into the first team squad he was sold to Ipswich for £1.5 million in July 2009. Is currently on loan at Charlton Athletic.

MARTIN, Mick

Appearances: 43 Goals: 2 (1972-1975)
Career: *Manchester United, WBA, Newcastle U, Cardiff City, Peterborough United, Rotherham United, Preston (1972-1985).* A £20,000 signing by Tommy Docherty from Irish outfit Bohemians, he initially helped the club beat the drop only to lose his place the following season when the relegation trap door opened below them. He failed to hold down a regular place in the promotion winning side and was sold to WBA, managed by Johnny Giles,. Has since coached both Newcastle and Celtic, and has been working as a radio pundit in the north east.

MATTHEWS, Sir Stanley

Appearances: 1 Goals: 0
Career: *Manchester United war time guest.* The wizard of dribble only played one game for United in June 1940 and ended up on the losing side in a 3-0 defeat to Everton. He tried his hand at management with Port Vale before travelling the world coaching and making guest appearances. He settled in Stoke-on-Trent, where he lived until his death in February 2000, aged 85, after falling ill on holiday in Spain.

Sir Stanley Matthews
Photo: chelsea_steve

MAY, David

Appearances: 118 Goals: 8 (1994-2003)
Career: *Blackburn Rovers, Manchester United, Huddersfield Town, Burnley (1988-2004).* A £1.2 million signing from Blackburn Rovers in the summer of 1994, mainly as a right back due to injuries to Paul Parker, until the emergence of Gary Neville. But then became a regular towards the end of his second season and after Steve Bruce departed to Birmingham, he cemented a regular place. He suffered from injuries but played a part in the charge to the treble after earlier being part of the double winning side. He remained at United in 2003 but mainly as a reserve after a string of injuries. He only won two Premier League winner's medals despite being part of six winning squads. May went on to become a part-time golfer as well as taking a job for a company that imports South African wine. He also works as a football television pundit and co-commentator for Manchester United's own TV station MUTV, and runs a company called United Nights which run "meet the player" events.

McALISTER, Luke

Appearances: 0 Goals: 0
Career: *Manchester United.* The son of a rugby league star, was a member of United's Academy as a youngster until returning to New Zealand to complete his schooling, where he started to play Rugby Union. Following a stint at Sale Sharks, the All Blacks fly half is now back in New Zealand playing for the Blues and North Harbour.

McCALLIOG, Jim

Appearances: 38 Goals: 7 (1973-1974)
Career: *Chelsea, Sheffield W, Wolves, Manchester United, Southampton, Lincoln City (1964-1978).* A £60,000 signing from Wolves on deadline day, March 1974, in a last ditch attempt to stave off relegation. He scored three goals in three games to give United some hope during a six match unbeaten run, but losing the last three games 1-0 saw them relegated. He played 20 games in the promotion winning season before losing his place, and had departed for Southampton before promotion was secured. Capped five times by Scotland, had spells as manager at Halifax Town and Runcorn, but then became a journalist and publican in Wetherby and York. He now has a pub in Fenwick, Ayrshire.

McCLAIR, Brian

Appearances: 471 Goals: 127 (1987-1998) Career: *Aston Villa, Manchester United (1980-1998).* Arrived at Old Trafford from Glasgow Celtic in July 1987 for £850,000 in a move south that proved fruitful. His first season brought 24 goals, the first United player to score 20 goals in a season since George Best 20 years previously. He formed a lethal partnership after a slow start with Mark Hughes, he scored the only goal in the 1992 League Cup Final, he was pushed back into midfield after the arrival of Eric Cantona but his chances became fewer when Roy Keane was signed. By the time he retired, he had won four

Premier League titles, three FA Cups, a League Cup, five Charity Shields and a UEFA Cup Winners Cup. In 1998, McClair joined Blackburn Rovers as assistant manager before returning to United to become a youth team coach. He also held the position of reserve team manager before being appointed Academy director in 2006.

McCREERY, David

Appearances: 110 Goals:8 (1975-79)
Career: *Manchester United, Queens Park Rangers, Newcastle United, Hartlepool United (1974-1995).* Was regularly used as an effective substitute during his stay at Old Trafford after being discovered by Northern Ireland scout, Billy Behan. Made his debut during the Second Division promotion winning season, a sub in the 1976 and 1977 FA Cup Finals, he earned the nickname of 'Roadrunner' for his endless running. But he could never quite hold down a regular place in the starting line and left to link up with Tommy Docherty at QPR in a £200,000 deal in August 1979. Northern Ireland international, managed Hartlepool and Carlisle and was a consultant for Major League Soccer and Boca Juniors. Is now a successful businessman in County Durham owning welding consumables company, Weldmore Ltd, and cutting tools distributor, Tallentire Tooling Ltd.

McDONAGH, Jim

Appearances: 0 Goals: 0 (1973)
Career: *Rotherham United, Manchester United, Bolton Wanderers, Everton, Bolton Wanderers, Notts County, Birmingham City, Sunderland, Gillingham, Scarborough, Huddersfield Town, Charlton Athletic (1970-1989).* A goalkeeper who was signed on loan from Rotherham United but never played a first team game, and returned to his home town club. Player manager of Galway and became a goalkeeping coach, has worked for a number of clubs and is now at Aston Villa.

McDONALD, Ken

Appearances: 9 Goals: 2 (1922-1924)
Career: *Cardiff City, Manchester United, Bradford City, Halifax Town (1921-1930)*. Made his United debut against Southampton in March 1923, he had to wait until the start of the 1923-1924 season before he really made his mark, opening the season with a goal after just two minutes against Bristol City. But he was unable to build on the foundations that he started to put down and along with Joe Myerscough, was sold to Bradford City for a combined fee of £1,500, going on to become a legend with 135 goals in 145 appearances. Was employed as a painter and decorator on Tyneside.

McFARLANE, Noel

Appearances: 1 Goals: 0 (1954-1956)
Career: *Manchester United (1954-1956)*. Signed by United in 1952, scoring twice the following year in the first leg of the FA Youth Cup Final success, but couldn't make his mark in the star studded first team squad. Johnny Berry kept him in the reserves and he only once made the first team for a 2-0 victory over Spurs in February 1954. He now lives in retirement in Alderley Edge, Cheshire, after working for the family of his wife in their wholesale fruit business at Manchester's Smithfields Market. His son, Ross, is a former professional golfer and now works for Sky.

McGARVEY, Scott

Appearances: 25 Goals: 3 (1980-1984)
Career: *Manchester United, Wolverhampton Wanderers, Portsmouth, Carlisle United, Grimsby Town, Bristol City, Oldham Athletic, Wigan Athletic (1980-1989)*. Tipped for a big future when he broke into the first team during Ron Atkinson's first season in charge, but then his Old Trafford career stalled when Norman Whiteside came through. He was loaned out to Wolves and then sold to Portsmouth for £85,000 in July 1984. Lived in Scotland, setting up his own company, Moneystone, which sold sand to sports clubs and agricultural concerns. He then moved to Prestwich, working as a football agent and a business consultant, now manager of Manchester Maccabi.

Photo: United Nights

McGIBBON, Pat

Appearances: 1 Goals: 0 (1995-1997)
Career: *Portadown, Manchester United, Swansea City, Wigan Athletic, Scunthorpe United, Tranmere Rovers (1991-2006).* Was signed for £100,000 from Northern Ireland based outfit Portadown, made his debut in the League Cup against York City but unfortunately he got himself sent off. He made the bench a number of times without getting a sniff of the action. He was loaned out to Swansea and Wigan who later paid United an initial £250,000 for his services. McGibbon is the assistant manager of Irish club, Monaghan United, having retired in 2006.

McGLEN, Billy

Appearances: 110 Goals: 2 (1946-1952)
Career: *Manchester United, Lincoln City, Oldham Athletic (1946-1953).* Steady performer picked up from non-league Blyth Spartans, he was recommended to Sir Matt Busby after being spotted playing services football in Italy, and he became his second ever signing. He was regular left back until cartilage trouble kept him out of action. He became outside left after Charlie Mitten left for Bogota, but after slipping into the reserves he was sold to Lincoln City in 1952 for £8,000. He lived in Manchester until retiring to Lincolnshire, where he died in December 1999.

McGRATH, Chris

Appearances: 34 Goals: 1 (1976-1981)
Career: *Tottenham Hotspur, Millwall, Manchester United (1973-1980).* Moved to Old Trafford for £30,000 in a bid to revive his career. Mainly used as a sub during his stay at the club, he enjoyed his best run under Dave Sexton but he couldn't get a regular run of games. His contract was cancelled in February 1981 to allow him to move to States. A former Northern Ireland international, worked at an armaments factory before moving to Glaxo-SmithKline in Herts.

Photo: Sporting Memorabilia

McGRATH, Paul

Appearances: 199 Goals: 16 (1982-1989) Career: *St Patricks Athletic, Manchester United, Aston Villa, Derby County, Sheffield United (1981-1998).* Spotted by Ron Atkinson and quickly snapped up for only £30,000 from Dublin side, St Patrick's. Had it not been for injuries and personal problems, Paul would have added to his haul of Republic of Ireland caps and United appearances. However, his undoubted ability enabled him to play on long after most of his peers had retired, but he only had a FA Cup Final victory against Everton, when he was voted Man Of The Match, to show for his years at Old Trafford. Often regarded as one of the best defenders in the game, he clashed with Sir Alex Ferguson because of his alcohol addiction. He rejected a retirement package of £100,000 plus a testimonial to retire. Instead he went to Aston Villa to continue his career. McGrath now lives in Monageer, County Wexford, in his native Republic of Ireland. His autobiography that dealt with his alcoholism as a player, named "Back from the Brink", was the most successful Irish sports book ever.

McGUINNESS, Paul

*Appearances: 0 Goals: 0 (1984-1986)
Career: Manchester United, Crewe
Alexandra, Manchester United, Bury,
Chester City (1984-1992).* McGuinness
progressed through the youth ranks at
Old Trafford but was unable to break
through into the first team squad, and
was allowed to join Crewe Alexandra.
Returned to Old Trafford in charge of
welfare and accommodation of youth
players, then became Director of
United's Centre of Excellence for 12
years before taking over the Under-18s
in the summer of 2005.

McGUINNESS, Wilf

*Appearances: 85 Goals: 2 (1955-1960)
Career: Manchester United (1955-1959).*
A Manchester born lad who looked to
be on the verge of a long and successful
career until he broke his leg at the age
of 22. He made his debut as a 17 year
old, he qualified for a League
Championship medal in his first season.
He missed the Munich air crash
because of cartilage problems. He was
playing the football of his life when he
badly broke a leg in a Central League
game at Old Trafford but despite a
comeback attempt, he was unable to
play again. Wilf stayed at Old Trafford
initially as a youth team coach, then later
as a reserve team coach and briefly
even became manager. Coached and
scouted for Everton, York, Hull, Bury and
the England youth team as well as United.
Now lives in Timperley and is a popular
speaker on the after dinner circuit.

MCILROY, Sammy

*Appearances: 419 Goals: 71 (1971-
1982) Career: Manchester United, Stoke
City, Manchester City, Bury, Preston
(1971-1989).* Another fine import from
across the Irish Sea, spotted as a
youngster by Matt Busby and he
became his last signing for the club, the
last ever Busby Babe. Once he had
signed professional terms, Sammy made
an immediate impact, scoring on his
debut in a local derby against City in
1971. Serious injuries in 1973 stopped
his progress for a while but he happily
returned to help the club to a Second
Division title and three FA Cup Finals. In
his 11 years at Old Trafford, he was fully
committed to the cause before being
allowed to leave for Stoke City in a
£350,000 transfer. Took Macclesfield
Town into the Football League, has
managed Northern Ireland, Stockport
and Morecombe since 2005 taking them
into the League.

McILVENNY, Ed

*Appearances: 2 Goals: 0 (1950-1951)
Career: Wrexham, Manchester United
(1947-1953).* Was Scotland born but he
still captained the USA to their shock
1950 World Cup win over England in
Belo Horizonte. He joined United after
his World Cup heroics and played in the
opening two games of the 1950-1951
season, making his debut against
Fulham in August 1950. Following a
defeat to Liverpool, he lost his place to
Don Gibson. Despite being on United's
books for another three years, he was
never given another chance in the first
team squad. Left United to become the
player manager of Waterford United in
Ireland. He later ran a soccer school,
died in Eastbourne in 1989, aged 64.

McKAY, Bill

*Appearances: 184 Goals: 15 (1933-
1940) Career: Bolton Wanderers,
Manchester United (1929-1940).* Played
his first game for Bolton against United
and when he became one of four
deadline day signings in March 1934, he
found himself pitched straight into a
relegation battle from Division Two. He
played a full part in winning the Second
Division title two years later, his career
was interrupted by the Second World
War. He worked in Trafford Park after the
War and was a regular at Old Trafford.

McKEE, Colin

Appearances: 0 Goals: 0 (1992-1994)
Career: *Manchester United, Bury (1992-1994).* Joined United as a trainee in 1989, a FA Youth Cup winner in 1992 alongside the likes of Ryan Giggs and David Beckham. After signing a professional contract in August 1992, he spent a month on loan at Bury, made his only first team appearance in May 1994 against Coventry City, and four months later was sold to Kilmarnock with Neil Whitworth in a combined deal worth £350,000. Lives in Carmyle, Glasgow, and works as a maintenance man for a building company and coaches part-time in Kilmarnock's Academy.

McKEOWN, Lindsay

Appearances: 0 Goals: 0 (1974-1976)
Career: *Manchester United, Sheffield Wednesday (1974-1979).* The Northern Ireland school boy international was discovered by United's legendary scout, Bob Bishop, who discovered George Best. He was signed from Linfield Rangers in July 1974, but he couldn't make the break through into the first team squad despite being a regular for the reserves in the two seasons that he spent at Old Trafford. After being given a free transfer in November 1976, he joined Sheffield Wednesday. Spent a number of years on the back room staff of Linfield before quitting in 1996 to work for Radio Ulster, which he combined with being an electrical sales rep, a job he started in 1985.

McKINNON, Rob

Appearances: 0 Goals: 0 (1990)
Career: *Newcastle United, Hartlepool United, Manchester United, Hartlepool United, Carlisle United (1985-2000).* A left back who was signed on loan from Hartlepool in 1990 but left without playing first team game. Is back in Scotland working in the family commercial vehicle repair and car body shop business in Paisley. He also does stats for the Press Association.

McLOUGHLIN, Alan

Appearances: 0 Goals: 0 (1983-1986)
Career: *Manchester United, Swindon Town, Torquay United, Southampton, Aston Villa, Portsmouth, Wigan Athletic, Rochdale (1985-2002).* Joined United as a trainee straight from school in 1983, and signed professional terms two years later. But he never made the breakthrough into the first team squad and was allowed to join Swindon in August 1986. Flourished 'down south' and became a regular Republic of Ireland international and was subject of a £1million move to Southampton in December 1990. became player-coach at Forest Green but when he finally hung up his boots he settled in Wiltshire and was a familiar voice on Portsmouth FC's Quay Radio until it closed in August 2010. He has also scouted for Nottingham Forest as well as running a soccer clinic and summer soccer schools.

Alan McLoughlin
Photo: Jake Payne

McMILLAN, Sammy

Appearances: 15 Goals: 6 (1961-1963)
Career: *Manchester United, Wrexham, Southend United, Chester City, Stockport County (1961-1971).* A youngster with outstanding promise, he progressed into the first team squad and scored 6 goals in 11 games, including braces against Leicester City and Sheffield United. But faced with stiff competition for places, despite his scoring record, he was allowed to join Wrexham on Christmas Eve 1963 for a fee of £8,000. A Northern Ireland international, became a process worker, living and working near Wrexham.

McNULTY, Tommy

Appearances: 57 Goals: 0 (1949-1954)
Career: *Manchester United, Liverpool (1947-1958).* An outstanding youngster who played 23 games during the 1951-1952 title winning season, when he partnered Roger Byrne at full back only to lose his place when Bill Foulkes emerged from the junior ranks, and he was sold to Liverpool in February 1954 for £7,000. He died in 1979, aged just 49.

McPHERSON, Frank

Appearances: 175 Goals: 52 (1923-1928)
Career: *Barrow, Manchester United, Watford, Reading, Watford, Barrow (1922-1937).* Signed by United just before his 21st birthday but had to spend the whole of his first season at Old Trafford playing in the reserves. Switching to centre forward saw him score 16 goals in 1925-1926, when the club returned to the First Division. Then the following season, he managed 16 goals. After six years at the club and following a brief spell with Manchester Central, he was sold to Watford for £850, proving to be a huge success at Vicarage Road. At the time of his sudden death in Davyholme, in March 1953, he was the licensee of the Greaves Arms Hotel in Oldham.

Photo: Gordonm1

McQUEEN, Gordon

Appearances: 229 Goals: 26 (1977-1985)
Career: *Leeds United, Manchester United (1970-1984).* Already an experienced Scottish international when United paid Leeds £495,000 for his services in February 1978, a month after Dave Sexton had been shopping at Elland Road for Joe Jordan. The 6ft 3in defender provided the club with seven years of invaluable service before being given a free transfer in 1985, by which time he'd scored in the 1979 FA Cup Final defeat to Arsenal. He was a Wembley winner four years later against Brighton, having lost in the League Cup Final earlier the same season. Managed Airdrie and worked for STV, before becoming reserve team coach at Middlesbrough. Then returned to television as a pundit on Sky Sports, is currently living in Hutton Rudby in North Yorkshire and works as an assistant scout at the Riverside.

Harry McShane with wife and future
international TV & film star son, Ian.
Photo: mcshanebest

McSHANE, Harry

Appearances: 57 Goals: 8 (1950-1954)
Career: *Blackburn Rovers, Huddersfield
Town, Bolton Wanderers, Manchester
United, Oldham Athletic (1937-1954).*
Arrived at Old Trafford in a swap deal
which took John Ball to Bolton
Wanderers. He replaced Charlie Mitten
at outside left and was a regular as
United finished runners up to Tottenham
Hotspur. The next season, he played 12
games as United won the title before
suffering a knee injury. He was sold to
Oldham for £750 on the eve on his 34th
birthday. Footballing father of Ian, star
of the BBC series 'Lovejoy'. Scouted for
Manchester United discovering Andy
Ritchie, Nicky Butt, Wes Brown among
others. Lives in Urmston and had
previously spent sixteen years working
for Massey Fergusons as a Personnel
Officer in Stretford until his retirement.
Was also a very popular tannoy announcer
at Old Trafford during the 1960s.

McSHANE, Paul

Appearances: 0 Goals: 0 (2004-2007)
Career: *Manchester United, Walsall,
Brighton, WBA, Sunderland, Hull City
(2004-2010).* Joined United as a trainee
in 2002 and twelve months later was a
FA Youth Cup winner. But never broke
into the first team squad and left for
WBA with Luke Steele as part of the
deal which bought Tomasz Kuszczah to
Old Trafford. The Republic of Ireland
international moved to Hull City for an
undisclosed fee in August 2007.

MEREDITH, Billy

*Appearances: 332 Goals: 35 (1906-
1921) Career: Manchester City,
Manchester United, Manchester City
(1894-1924).* The legendary Welsh
international who never played without a
tooth pick, came to United after his
contract across the City was cancelled
after he was banned in an illegal
payments scandal. He was made to wait
until New Year's Day 1907 for his ban to
be lifted so he could make his debut.
He helped the club to two League titles
and a FA Cup, and it wasn't until he was
47 that he was given a free transfer, only
for him to return to City as player coach
and continue playing until after his 50th
birthday. He was one of the first
members of the Players' Union, he also
had a career as a sports outfitter but the
business went bust in the year he joined
United. He later became the licensee of
a cinema and Manchester publican, and
was also on United's coaching staff for a
while. He died in Withington,
Manchester, in April 1958, aged 83.

METTRICK, Mark

Appearances: 0 Goals: 0 (1982-1984)
Career: *Manchester United (1982-
1984).* A Manchester born midfielder
who spent two years in United's youth
team, he was offered a professional
contract but instead opted to move to
New York to continue his education at
Hartwick College, where he also played
for their football team. He stayed in the
States after working for Mount St. Mary's
University. Has been head coach at
Loyola College in Maryland for the last
decade.

MEW, Jack

Appearances: 199 Goals: 0 (1912-1926)
Career: *Manchester United, Barrow (1912-1927).* A goalkeeper who served United for 14 years, becoming the first player to receive two benefits from the club. The first netted him £1,000 but the second was capped at £650. It was after the Great War when he made his mark, only missing four games in four seasons, and with his full back partners Charlie Moore and Jack Silcock, he clocked up an impressive run of 26 consecutive games. He left the club for Barrow three years later. He went into business with Lancashire and England cricketer, Cecil Parkin, before coaching in Belgium and Peru. He settled in Stretford and worked in a Manchester factory. He died in October 1963, aged 74.

MICKLEWHITE, Gary

Appearances: 0 Goals: 0 (1978-1979)
Career: *Manchester United, Queens Park Rangers, Derby County, Gillingham (1978-1996).* He spent a season at Old Trafford as a professional without making the breakthrough into the first team squad, and was signed by Tommy Docherty when he took over the reigns at Queens Park Rangers. He was youth development officer at QPR, assistant manager at Wycombe and a coach with Charlton. Is now a cab driver in London

MILLER, Liam

Appearances: 22 Goals: 2 (2004-2006)
Career: *Manchester United, Leeds United, Sunderland, QPR (2004-2009).* Joined United on a free transfer from Celtic in July 2004, he made his debut in a Champions League clash with Dinamo Bucharest, with his first goal arriving in a League Cup tie with Crewe in October 2004. But he found his chances limited, spending most of 2005-2006 season on loan at Leeds United. In August 2006, he was allowed to leave United on a free transfer to join Roy Keane's Sunderland. In September 2009, he moved back to Scotland to play for Hibs.

MILNE, Ralph

Appearances: 30 Goals: 3 (1988-1990)
Career: *Charlton Athletic, Bristol City, Manchester United, West Ham United (1977-1989).* A surprise £175,000 signing to succeed Jesper Olsen on the left flank, never popular with the Old Trafford crowd he faded from the scene, after a season on loan at West Ham failed to spark life into his career. He was released on a free transfer and ended his career with a spell in Hong Kong. Ran a pub in Bristol for a decade and battled drink and gambling addictions. Returned to Dundee and has done a number of jobs including a lorry driver.

MITTEN, Charlie

Appearances: 161 Goals: 61 (1946-1950) Career: *Manchester United, Fulham, Mansfield Town (1938-1958).* Born in Rangoon while his father was serving there in the army, Mitten proved himself to be an adept winger and goal scorer, once scoring three penalties in a match against Aston Villa. A FA Cup winner in 1948, two years later he was tempted to take the fortune offered by a Columbian club earning him his nickname the "Bogota Bandit". However, he was back at Old Trafford within a year despite being offered more money by Real Madrid. He was banned for six months by Sir Matt Busby, transfer listed and promptly sold to Fulham. He managed Mansfield and Newcastle United before becoming the manager of the White City Greyhound Stadium in Manchester. He later ran a sports promotions firm. He lived in Stockport in his retirement and died in January 2002, two weeks short of his 81st birthday.

MOGER, Harry

*Appearances: 264 Goals: 0 (1903-1912)
Career: Southampton, Manchester United (1900-1912).* Spent his first season at the club in the reserves and seemed to suffer from nerves when given a chance to impress on the big stage, but that all changed when he saved a penalty against Burslem (Port Vale). For the next seven seasons, he was first choice goalkeeper in a golden era which bought the club two League titles and a FA Cup. Despite the success, he couldn't ever break into the England side. He had worked as a fitter before turning professional but worked as a commercial agent after his playing days. He died in June 1927, aged only 47.

MOIR, Ian

*Appearances: 45 Goals: 5 (1960-1965)
Career: Manchester United, Blackpool, Chester City, Wrexham, Shrewsbury Town, Wrexham (1960-1975).* Scotsman who began as a United amateur, made his first team debut at Bolton Wanderers in October 1960 alongside Nobby Stiles. His best season came in 1963-1964 when United finished runners up to Liverpool. But the emergence of George Best and John Connolly saw him relegated to the reserves and he was sold to Blackpool. Worked as a lecturer in sports sociology at the University of Birmingham's School of Sports and Exercise Sciences.

MONCUR, Bobby

Career: Newcastle United, Sunderland, Carlisle United (1962-1976). Joined United on trial in the early 1960s as a youngster but was never offered terms after he became homesick. Managed Carlisle, Hearts, Plymouth and Hartlepool, opened a squash club, worked in insurance and hospitality, ran his own yacht charter business in Newcastle. Is now a radio pundit for Century FM and also seen on Sky Sports.

MOORE, Graham

*Appearances: 19 Goals: 5 (1963-1964)
Career: Cardiff City, Chelsea, Manchester United, Northampton Town, Charlton Athletic, Doncaster Rovers (1958-1973).* Signed by Sir Matt Busby from Tommy Docherty's Chelsea for £35,000, a promising debut against Tottenham proved to be a false dawn as he spent two unproductive seasons at Old Trafford and struggled to hold down a regular first team place. He was allowed to leave for Northampton Town to kick-start his career. The Welsh international midfielder also played for Charlton Athletic and Doncaster Rovers, before running a pub at Easingwold and then a sub post office in Scarborough . He now lives in retirement in the North Yorkshire village of Burythorpe Malton, next door to the pub he used to run.

MORAN, Kevin

Appearances: 289 Goals: 24 (1978-1988) Career: Manchester United, Blackburn Rovers (1978-1994). An accomplished gaelic footballer who managed to maintain the passion shown in his former sport whilst in the heart of United's back four. This unfortunately resulted in Kevin receiving more than his fair share of cuts and bruises, earning him the nickname 'Captain Blood' in the tabloid press. He was spotted by United's legendary Irish talent spotter, Billy Behan, and became a regular in the United team throughout the 1980s, winning two FA Cup winner's medals. He was the first player to be sent off in a FA Cup Final in 1985. He moved to Sporting Gijon of Spain when given a free transfer from United in 1988 but returned to England for a spell with Blackburn Rovers. Republic of Ireland central defender, retired at the end of the 1993-4 season. Became a players agent after forming Proactive Sports Management with Jesper Olsen, and is also a television pundit in Ireland.

MORGAN, Willie

Appearances: 238 Goals: 25
Career: Burnley, Manchester United, Burnley, Bolton Wanderers, Blackpool (1962-1981). Converted by Frank O'Farrell from the wing to midfield, where he shone for the best part of six years. Originally recruited from Burnley for £100,000 in 1968 to take over from John Connolly, who he had replaced at Burnley when he moved to United, he took over from George Best wearing the number seven shirt. He helped United to the Second Division title before clashing with Tommy Docherty. He made the return trip to Turf Moor. Docherty later sued Morgan and Granada TV for libel but later withdrew it after admitting that he lied under oath and was ordered to pay £30,000 costs. Retired from the game having invested his money in a chain of laundrettes. Briefly opened a sports shop in Altrincham. Lives in Wilmslow and is the boss of a marketing company, MSB Marketing.

Kenny Morgans at Albert Scanlon's funeral.
Photo: Stephen Broadhurst

MORGANS, Kenny

Appearances: 23 Goals: 0 (1957-1959)
Career: Manchester United, Swansea City, Newport County (1957-1967). A member of back-to-back FA Youth Cup winning sides, a promising winger he made his league debut in the same game as Harry Gregg against Leicester in December 1957. He then survived the Munich air crash but was never the same player afterwards. The harrowing effects of what happened appeared to leave deep scars and despite making a quick comeback, he only played four games in the next two seasons and was sold to Swansea City for a nominal £3,000 fee. He became a publican in Pontypool, then a salesman, before retiring.

MORRIS, Johnny

Appearances: 83 Goals: 32 (1946-1949)
Career: Manchester United, Derby County, Leicester City (1941-1958). Born in Radcliffe, John played for the juniors before signing professional terms in 1941. He had to wait until the end of the Second World War for his career to take off but then he won a FA Cup winner's medal in his first season in 1948. United finished First Division runners up in the same season, and his contribution was an impressive haul of 21 goals in 44 appearances. He fell out with Sir Matt Busby after he was left out of the team in early 1949, and after handing in a transfer request, he left Old Trafford for Derby County in a record breaking deal worth £24,500. An England international, he won three caps and scored on his debut in a match against Norway and notched up two more in his next appearance against France. Later managed several non-league teams including Corby Town, Kettering , Rugby and Oswestry. Became a tyre salesman after leaving the game in 1969.

MOSES, Remi

Appearances: 199 Goals: 12 (1981-1988) Career: West Bromwich Albion, Manchester United (1979-1988). Remi Moses' signature for the club in 1981 was significant on two counts. For Manchester born Remi, it was a homecoming. For the club, it meant buying the first black player to pull on the famous jersey for a league match. The £650,000 paid to West Bromwich albion purchased a tenacious England Under 23 midfielder. His United career was hit by injury and bad luck. A sending off against Arsenal cost him a place in the 1983 FA Cup Final, and sadly he was forced to quit through injury when only 27, with only a League Cup runners up medal to show for his efforts. Since retiring from the game he has been spending his time buying and selling properties in Manchester and has coached an inline skating team. Has also coached for a Community group, Unity, in the Community running Old Trafford FC.

MUHREN, Arnold

Appearances: 98 Goals: 18 (1982-1985) Career: Ipswich Town, Manchester United (1978-1984). A stylish Dutch international who graced Old Trafford after making his mark at Ipswich Town, where he had been part of the 1981 UEFA cup winning team. He joined United in 1982 after his contract at Portman Road had run out. He helped United win the FA Cup in his first season at the club, scoring the fourth goal in the 4-0 victory over Brighton. United were in the running for the title in his second season until he was injured in March and he was while sidelined, their challenge faded dramatically. The injuries started to trouble him and he was never able to hold down a regular place in the side again. Now lives back in Holland, where he worked for Volendam coaching youngsters, and is now working for one of his former clubs, Ajax of Amsterdam, coaching a youth team.

Photo: Leslie Millman

MULRYNE, Philip

Appearances: 5 Goals: 0 (1997-1999)
Career: *Manchester United, Norwich City, Cardiff City, Leyton Orient (1996-2007).* A member of United's 1995 FA Youth Cup winning team, he made his international debut for Northern Ireland against Belgium 11 months before he made his first team bow against Ipswich in the Coca Cola Cup. But with many big name stars in front of him, he only managed to play a handful of first team games before he joined Norwich City for £500,000, in March 1999, in a bid to secure himself more first team football. Was invited by the Bishop of Down and Connor to enter the priesthood and in seven years, he could be ordained as a priest for the diocese.

MURDOCK, Colin

Appearances: 0 Goals: 0 (1991-1997)
Career: *Manchester United, Preston NE, Crewe A, Rotherham U, Shrewsbury Town, Accrington Stanley (1991-2009).* A member of United's FA Youth Cup runners up side of 1993, two years after he joined the club as a school leaver. He was offered a professional contract 12 months later but was never able to make the breakthrough into the first team picture, and was sold to Preston in May 1997 for £165,000. The former Northern Ireland international is now a sports lawyer with Manchester firm, George Davies LLP, and is a member of the FA Football Judicial Panel.

MURPHY, Aidan

Appearances: 0 Goals: 0 (1984-1987)
Career: *Manchester United, Lincoln City, Oldham Athletic, Crewe Alexandra, Scarborough (1986-1993).* Worked his way through the ranks at Old Trafford, but never realised his potential, which bought him England youth and schoolboy honours. He had one season as a professional with loan spells at Lincoln City and Oldham Athletic before being released to spend five years playing for Crewe Alexandra. Started work for the Greensboro Youth Soccer in 1998 and three years later was appointed Boys Youth Development Director for GYS. He has also been on the staff of the NCYSA olympic development program since Spring 2000. He moved to the South Charlotte Soccer Association in May 2006 but returned to Greensboro due to his family not settling in his new location, and is assistant director of coaching.

MUSTOE, Neil

Appearances: 0 Goals: 0
Career: *Manchester United, Wigan Athletic, Cambridge United, Yeovil Town (1995-2003).* Joined United in 1995 as a schoolboy, winning a FA Youth Cup winner's medal two years later. He was awarded a professional contract but was released by Sir Alex Ferguson without playing a first team game. Since 2003, he has been back in his native Gloucester playing for a local non-league team and working in a warehouse in the Gloucester Business Park.

MUTCH, George

Appearances: 120 Goals: 49 (1934-1938) Career: *Manchester United, Preston North End, Bury, Southport (1934-1948).* His United career exploded into life three games after his £800 move from Arbroath, when he scored a five minute hat trick against Barnsley in September 1934. He was the leading scorer with 21 goals in 42 games when United were crowned Division Two Champions two years later. He was sold to powerful Preston for £5,000 in September 1937. Had a two year spell as trainer at Southport after he finished his career after leaving Haigh Avenue. He returned to his native Aberdeen to open a grocery business and later worked as a PT instructor. He died in March 2001, aged 88.

MYERSCOUGH, Joe

Appearances: 34 Goals: 8 (1920-1923)
Career: *Manchester United, Bradford Park Avenue (1920-1927)*. The winner of a Central League Championship medal in his first season at the club, he made his first team debut against Bolton Wanderers in September 1920, but then dropped out of the side for 16 games. On his return, he scored four goals in a week. Both games were against Bradford PA, the team he eventually joined along with Kenneth MacDonald for a combined fee of £1,500. He became a painter and decorator in Lancaster, died in Scotforth, near Lancaster, in July 1975, aged 81.

NARDIELLO, Daniel

Appearances: 4 Goals: 0 (2000-2005)
Career: *Manchester United, Swansea C, Barnsley, QPR, Barnsley, Blackpool, Hartlepool U, Bury, Oldham A, Exeter C (2000-2010)*. A product of the Wolves Academy, and United were ordered to pay £200,000 compensation when they signed him in 1999. He made his first team debut in a League Cup tie against Arsenal in November 2001 but he was released four years later, after failing to become a regular in the first team, and joined Blackpool. The son of former Coventry City winger, Donato Nardiello, he signed for Exeter City in July 2010 after being released by Blackpool.

NEUMAYR, Markus

Appearances: 0 Goals: 0 (2003-2006)
Career: *Manchester United (2003-2006)*. Signed as a youngster from Eintracht Frankfurt in 2003. He was made reserve team captain following David Fox's transfer to Blackpool. It only seemed a matter of time before he broke into the first team squad but it never happened, and he asked to be released from his contract in 2006 to join Duisburg. He has led a nomadic career since leaving Old Trafford and in April 2010, announced he had joined Wacker Burghausen.

Photo: illarterate

NEVILLE, Phil

Appearances: 386 Goals: 8 (1994-2005)
Career: *Manchester United, Everton (1994-date)*. Younger of the two Neville brothers, Phil excelled from the moment he made his debut and was awarded his first England cap at the age of 19. Suffered from an ankle injury and then from glandular fever, he managed to recover both his health and his brilliant form. He won six Premier League titles, three FA Cups and the European Cup before signing for Everton in August 2005. Is still in the first team squad at Goodison Park.

NICHOLL, Jimmy

Appearances: 248 Goals: 5 (1974-1982)
Career: *Manchester United, Sunderland, WBA (1974-1985)*. Born in Canada, made his league debut in 1974. He battled Alex Forsyth for the right back spot until making the position his own. He was a first team regular until Ron Atkinson took over as boss from Dave Sexton, and immediately signed John Gidman from Everton. Nicholl never got a look in again and was sold to Toronto Blizzard for £250,000. A former Northern Ireland international, has twice managed Raith Rovers and Millwall. In June 2010, he became manager of Cowdenbeath.

NICHOLSON, Jimmy

Appearances: 68 Goals: 6 (1960-1963)
Career: *Manchester U, Huddersfield Town, Bury (1960-1975).* Discovered in Dublin by United scout Bob Harpur, his debut against Everton in August 1960 ended in a 4-0 defeat, the reverse fixture a week later saw him score in a 4-0 victory. Often compared to Duncan Edwards, which probably did him no favours, he spent five years on United's books before moving to Huddersfield for £8,000 in 1964. Had various jobs before becoming manager of Sale Sports Centre, just a few minutes walk from his home.

NOBLE, Bobby

Appearances: 33 Goals: 0 (1965-1969)
Career: *Manchester United (1962-1969).* A former Youth team mate of George Best, made his debut against Leicester in March 1966 and became a regular the following season. He looked set for an exceptional career until he suffered head and chest injuries in a car crash. He regained fitness but troubled by double vision and was advised to quit the game by a FA Medical Board two years after the accident. Now lives in Sale and worked for a Manchester printing company.

O'KANE, John

Appearances: 7 Goals: 0 (1994-1997)
Career: *Manchester United, Bury, Bradford C, Everton, Burnley, Bolton W, Blackpool (1993-2003).* A Nottingham born defender who was a member of United's 1991-1992 FA Youth Cup winning side. He signed a professional deal in 1993 as an 18 year old and his debut came in the League Cup against Port Vale in September 1994. He couldn't, however, hold down a regular place and was sold to Everton for £400,000 after two years in the Old Trafford wilderness. Quit football after leaving Hyde United in 2006 ,he now lives in Darwin, Lancashire, and works as a property developer.

O'KEEFE, Eamonn

Career: *Manchester United, Plymouth A, Everton, Wigan A, Port Vale, Blackpool, Chester City (1974-1990).* A United fan who grew up in Blackley, North Manchester. He spent two seasons at Old Trafford as a junior but was never offered terms and joined Stalybridge Celtic. Was once arrested by police on suspicion of being an IRA terrorist. Went to work for social services working in a residential units. Now lives in semi-retirement in Vilamoura on the Algarve, working for a property company.

O'BRIEN, Ray

Appearances: 0 Goals: 0 (1973)
Career: *Manchester United, Notts County, Derby County (1973-1983).* He started his career in Dublin with Shelbourne before moving to Old Trafford as part of the deal which bought Gerry Daly to the club. He never managed to break into the first team squad apart from one first team friendly in Scotland, and was allowed to leave without making an competitive appearance. Joined Notts County for £45,000. Became a reprographics manager with Nottinghamshire County Council, living in Nottingham, and works in the printing industry in Newark.

O'BRIEN, Liam

Appearances: 36 Goals: 2 (1986-1989)
Career: *Manchester United, Newcastle United, Tranmere Rovers (1986-1999).* A Ron Atkinson signing for £55,000, but it wasn't until Sir Alex Ferguson took control of first team affairs that he was given a chance to impress in the first team squad. He made seven full appearances and another two as a sub in his first season, but he rejected a new deal when he failed to get a regular start and made the £275,000 move to Newcastle United, in November 1988. A Republic of Ireland international, was once sent off after just 85 seconds. Has managed a number of clubs in Ireland where he runs a chauffeuring business.

OLIVE, Les
*Appearances: 2 Goals: 0 (1952-1953)
Career: Manchester United (1952-1953).*
Olive first became associated with the
club when he joined the ground staff at
the age of 14 straight from school. He
went on to play for United's five teams in
almost every position. His only two
league appearances were in March
1953 against Newcastle United and West
Bromwich Albion and were made in
goal, when the club's three goalkeepers,
Ray Wood, Jack Crompton and Reg
Allen, were all injured. He made his
debut on the same day as Dennis Viollet
and provided the club with their first
away win in four months. After only a
brief playing career, he was appointed
the club's assistant secretary in 1955.
Three years later he became one of the
youngest secretaries in the league when
his boss, Walter Crickmer, died in the
Munich air crash. Sadly, one of the first
tasks that he had to perform in his new
role was to inform the deceased players'
families of the tragedy and help to
organise the funerals. He kept his role
for 30 years before joining the board of
directors until 2005. He died the
following year, in May 2006, aged 78,
from prostrate cancer.

Jesper Olsen
*Photo: Preben T. A. Arentoft
(son of the former Newcastle player!)*

OLSEN, Jesper
*Appearances: 176 Goals: 24 (1984-
1988) Career: Manchester United (1984-
1988).* A Danish international winger,
born in Copenhagen, Olsen arrived at
Old Trafford via Amsterdam where he
had been a star with Ajax. Ron Atkinson
spotted his potential, paying around
£700,000 to bring him to England. On
his day, Olsen was magnificent. He
played in the 1985 FA Cup final against
Everton but lacked consistency, and
struggled to adapt to English football.
His fortunes improved under Sir Alex
Ferguson but he didn't last and was sold
to Bordeaux for £400,000 in November
1988. After his playing days, which had
earned him 40 international caps, the
Daner has kept a fairly low profile since
retiring. Lived in Alderley Edge,
Cheshire, and ran a sports management
company with Kevin Moran before
moving to Australia where he lives in
Brighton, Victoria. Suffered a brain
haemorrhage in 2006 and was taken to
hospital but has since made a good
recovery and is now an assistant coach
for Melbourne Heart in the Australian 'A'
League.

O'NEIL, Tommy
*Appearances:68 Goals: 0 (1971-1973)
Career: Manchester United, Blackpool,
Southport, Tranmere Rovers, Halifax,
Southport (1971-1982).* A dual
schoolboy international at both rugby
and football, he made his first team
debut in the last game of the 1970-1971
season, a 4-3 victory over Manchester
City under Frank O'Farrell. He was first
the Irish manager's first choice right
back but when Tommy Docherty gave
his place to Tony Young, he was sent out
on loan to Blackpool before being sold
to Southport. He went into coaching, and
returned to United to coach at their
Academy until shortly before his death
in May 2006, aged 53.

Photo: 1Goal (www.join1goal.org)

O'SULLIVAN, Peter

Appearances: 0 Goals:0 (1968-1970)
Career: *Manchester United, Brighton, Fulham, Charlton Athletic, Reading, Aldershot (1968-1983).* He progressed through the junior ranks to become an apprentice, before signing a professional contract in 1968. But unable to break into the star studded first team squad, O'Sullivan joined Brighton on a free transfer in April 1970. He worked in the building industry before selling insurance and now works for a Brighton plant hire company

PAGE, Louis

Appearances: 12 Goals: 0 (1932)
Career: *Stoke City, Northampton Town, Burnley, Manchester United, Port Vale (1919-1933).* Signed for £1,000 on transfer deadline day in March 1932, making his debut against Charlton Athletic in the same month. When A Scott Duncan was appointed first team boss, one of his first tasks was to name Page as his new captain but under two months into the new season, he was sold to Port Vale. Went into management and took charge of Newport County, Swindon Town for eight years, and Chester. Later scouted for Leicester City but died in Prenton, Birkenhead in October 1959, aged 60.

PALLISTER, Gary

Appearances: 437 Goals: 15 (1989-1997) Career: *Middlesbrough, Darlington, Manchester United, Middlesbrough (1984-2001).* Although born in Kent, Gary first proved his worth as an outstanding defender in the north east of the country, in Middlesbrough's colours. Their fans were shocked when a £2.3 million transfer fee persuaded the club to let Pally move to Old Trafford in August 1989. Problems with a back injury repeatedly proved irritating, not least when they resulted in him missing Euro 96. He was awarded the PFA

Player's Player of The Year award in 1991-1992 and by the time he left United, it was with four Premier League titles, three FA Cups, a League Cup, Cup Winners Cup, UEFA Cup and five Charity Shields safely in the trophy cabinet. Pallister was forced to retire in 2001, became television football pundit for the BBC and ITV. He joined Darlington in a commercial role as Operations Director in September 2010.

Paul Parker (3rd from left)
Photo: Lancs & Cheshire Amateur League

PARKER, Paul

Appearances: 146 Goals: 2 (1991-1996)
Career: *Fulham, Queens Park Rangers, Manchester United, Derby County, Sheffield United, Fulham, Chelsea (1982-1997).* A small but lightning fast defender procured from QPR for a fee of £1.7 million in August 1991, he made his debut in the same month as right back against Notts County. He struggled to maintain his fitness for his five years at the club, but he won trophies as Sir Alex Ferguson's United started to dominate the domestic game. He won two Premier League winner's medals as well as FA Cup and League Cups. But injuries and Gary Neville took their toll and he was allowed to leave for Derby County. Parker went on to manage Chelmsford City and Welling United before being named as ambassador for the Blue Square Premier League (Conference National). Parker has also worked as a television football pundit for Setanta Sports.

PATERSON, Steve

Appearances: 10 Goals: 0 (1974-1980)
Career: *Manchester United (1974-1980).* A product of junior football in the Highlands of Scotland, joined United as a 16 year old. He made his League debut against Sunderland in December 1976 but was released after a serious ankle injury. He never played league football in England again, after seeing a move to Sheffield Wednesday fall through when he failed a medical. Enjoyed a largely successful 15 year career in football management in Scotland, the majority of which was combined with a job as a social worker. Suffered with gambling and alcohol problems, is working as a social worker in a residential home.

PEARS, Stephen

Appearances: 5 Goals: 0 (1979-1985)
Career: *Manchester United, Middlesbrough, Liverpool, Hartlepool United (1979-1998).* He started his United career as understudy to Gary Bailey but he struggled to get a regular place in the starting line, and was sent to Middlesbrough for first team experience. After becoming a Fans' Favourite, they failed to match United's £80,000 asking price and he finally got a chance when Bailey broke a finger. But Boro raised the finance to secure his signature and he returned to Boro as Academy goalkeeping coach, and has since been promoted to coach the senior keepers at the club.

Photo: imedagoze

PEARSON, Mark

Appearances: 80 Goals: 14 (1957-1963)
Career: *Manchester United, Sheffield Wednesday, Fulham, Halifax Town (1957-1968).* The Sheffield boy nicknamed 'Pancho', due to his sideburns, initially joined as an amateur. Turned professional in 1957 and showed signs of becoming a natural successor to his famous namesake, Stan Pearson. He was sent off twice before his 19th birthday, he couldn't hold down a regular first team place because of injuries despite his early promise, and he returned to his home town to play for Sheffield Wednesday in a £22,500 deal. He stayed in Yorkshire and worked as a driller for a Bradford engineering company before going self-employed in 1994 until his retirement.

PEARSON, Stan

Appearances: 345 Goals: 149 (1937-1954) Career: *Manchester United, Bury, Chester City (1936-1959).* Salford born striker who played as an amateur before the war, then starred in the early Busby sides as a professional. Was one of several promising youngsters who helped United win promotion from the Second Division in his debut season, he lost six years to the war but his hat trick helped United into the 1948 FA Cup Final. He then scored a fine goal in the 4-2 win over Blackpool. He only missed 13 games in 7 seasons after the war and won eight England international caps and scored five goals for his country. Pearson eventually lost his place to Jackie Blanchflower after winning the League Championship in 1952, and was sold to Bury for £4,500. He also played for Chester City and managed the club from 1959 to1961. He later took on a newsagency in Prestbury becoming a sub postmaster. He died in Alderley Edge, Cheshire, in February 1997, aged 78.

Photo: Sporting Memorabilia

PEARSON, Stuart

Appearances: 139 Goals: 55 (1974-1979) Career: Hull City, Manchester United, West Ham United (1968-1982). Topped United's goal scoring charts three years in succession following his £200,000 move from Hull City, where he had also regularly been their top scorer. He was signed after relegation to the Second Division and his 17 goals helped the club back into the top flight at the first attempt. He became a firm fans' favourite at Old Trafford, was a member of the 1977 FA Cup winning side. He missed almost all of his last season at the club with a knee injury and after failing to agree terms with Tommy Docherty, left for West Ham United in a £220,000 deal. Played rugby union for Sale Sharks before he went into coaching with Stockport County, West Bromwich Albion and Bradford City. Now lives most of the year in Spain, but regularly returns to the UK to work for MUTV and to give legend tours of Old Trafford.

PEGG, Dave

Appearances: 148 Goals: 28 (1952-1958) Career: Manchester United (1952-1958). A pacey mobile winger who had made one full appearance for England, won two League Championship before his life was cut tragically short in Munich, which ironically came after he lost his place to Albert Scanlon but as a squad member, made the fateful trip to Belgrade. He was the left wing supplier of chances for Dennis Violet and Tommy Taylor. He played in successive FA Youth Cup winning teams. Dave was still only 22 at the time of the accident. He is buried in Redhouse Cemetery, near Doncaster where he was born.

PEMBERTON, John

Appearances: 0 Goals: 0 Career: Rochdale, Crewe Alexandra, Crystal Palace, Sheffield United, Leeds United, Crewe Alexandra (1984-1999). Joined United as a junior but was released without ever making an impression. He dropped into non-league football with Chadderton before returning to the league with Rochdale. Was on the coaching staff at Nottingham Forest and served as caretaker boss at the City Ground for a brief spell, he then had a stint at Crystal Palace until May 2010.

PENFOLD, Mark

Appearances: 0 Goals: 0 (1975) Career: Charlton Athletic, Manchester United, Leyton Orient, Maidstone United (1974-1983). The Woolwich born full back joined United on a month's loan in February 1975 with a view to a permanent deal, but he only managed to play a handful of games for the reserves during his short stint at Old Trafford. He returned to his parent club without playing any first team games. Mark is now manager of a cleaning company and a hospitality host at Charlton on matchdays, and is an active member of their former players' association.

PHELAN, Mike

Appearances: 145 Goals: 3 (1989-1994)
Career: *Burnley, Norwich City, Manchester United, WBA (1979-1995).* Good honest midfield performer signed by Alex Ferguson in the summer of 1989. Outstanding displays for Norwich City had earned him much respect and a £750,000 price tag, and he followed his Carrow Road team mate, Steve Bruce, to Old Trafford. He won a FA Cup winner's medal in his first season then followed it up with success in the Cup Winners Cup and League Cup. He was given a free transfer at the age of 33 when the likes of David Beckham and Nicky Butt threatened his place on the bench, after the younger generation took his place in the starting line up. Went into coaching with Norwich and Stockport before returning to Old Trafford to run the Centre of Excellence. Was promoted to first team coach then assistant manager in September 2008.

PICKEN, Phil

Appearances: 0 Goals: 0 (2002-2006)
Career: *Manchester United, Chesterfield, Notts County, Bury (2002-2010).* Joined United as a junior in 2002 and did well enough to be offered professional terms two seasons later. Hailing from Droylsden, he was part of the United's reserve team who won the quadruple in 2005. But he never progressed any further and was released to join Chesterfield. In the summer of 2010, he joined Bury.

PILKINGTON, Kevin

Appearances: 8 Goals: 0 (1994-1998)
Career: *Manchester United, Rochdale, Rotherham United, Port Vale, Wigan Athletic, Mansfield Town, Notts County, Luton Town (1992-2010).* A member of United's 1992 FA Youth, he made his debut when Peter Schmeichel was injured during a game with Crystal Palace in November 1994. The following season he made his first start in the League Cup tie against York City,

then his full league debut followed against Chelsea in December 1995. He stayed at Old Trafford for another three years without breaking into the first team on a regular basis, before joining Port Vale in June 1998 on a free transfer. In June 2010, he joined Luton Town after being released by Notts County. Also coaches at Sells Goalkeeping Academy.

PINNER, Mike

Appearances: 4 Goals: 0 (1960-1961)
Career: *Aston Villa, Sheffield Wednesday, Queens Park Rangers, Manchester United, Chelsea, Arsenal, Chelsea, Swansea City, Leyton Orient (1954-1965).* He was brought to United when Harry Gregg and Dave Gaskell were both sidelined. Third choice, Ronnie Briggs had conceded six goals on his debut and seven in his second game. Pinner stabilised the situation after making his debut at Old Trafford against Aston Villa in February 1961 but he only made a handful of appearances before the two first choice keepers were fit to take their place in the side, and he was allowed to move on. Worked as a solicitor for most his career, played in two Olympic Games, and was still working for the London law firm Hatchick Solicitors well into his 70s.

Gerard Pique

PIQUE, Gerard
Appearances:23 Goals: 2 (2004-2008)
Career: *Manchester United (2004-2008).*
Signed from Barcelona in 2004 for
nothing because he was too young to be
offered a professional contract. He
made his debut against Crewe in the
League Cup in the same season but he
had to wait until March 2006 to make his
full debut against West Ham. After
spending a season on loan at Real
Zaragoza, Pique spent another season at
United before returning to Barca in May
2008 for an undisclosed fee.

Photo: Omar Gurnah

PLATT, David
Appearances: 0 Goals: 0 (1982-1985)
Career: *Manchester United, Crewe
Alexandra, Aston Villa, Arsenal,
Nottingham Forest (1982-2001).* Joined
United as an apprentice after leaving
school in 1992, and did enough to earn
himself a professional contract in 1984-
1985 season but he failed to make an
impact, and was given a free transfer by
Ron Atkinson as part of a cost cutting
exercise in January 1985. He went on to
join Crewe, Alexandra growing into an
accomplished international midfielder.

Managed Sampdoria, Nottingham Forest
and the England Under-21 side. Then
worked as a television pundit. Is
currently back in the game as part of
Man City's back room team.

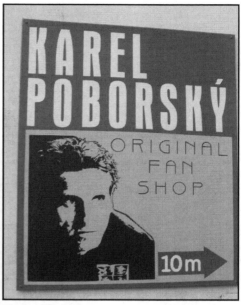

Photo: AlBakker

POBORSKY, Karel
Appearances: 32 Goals: 5(1996-1998)
Career: *Manchester United (1996-1998).*
Was only at Old Trafford for a season
and a half because his time at the club
coincided with the emergence of a
youngster called David Beckham. He
was signed for £3.5 million after a
worldwide search by Sir Alex Ferguson,
who had been looking to replace Andrei
Kanchelskis. He was dubbed the Czech
Express but was allowed to join Benfica
as he struggled to adjust to life in the
Premier League. Following his spell in
Portugal, he went on to play for Lazio in
Italy and then returned home to spend
three years playing for Sparta Prague.
He ended career in 2007 back at SK
Dynamo Èeské Budìjovice, the club
where had started some sixteen years
before. Poborsky is currently working as
a technical leader for the Czech
Republic international team.

POLLITT, Mike

Appearances: 0 Goals: 0 (1988-1991)
Career: *Manchester United, Oldham, Macclesfield T, Bury, Lincoln C, Darlington, Notts Co, Oldham A, Gillingham, Brentford, Sunderland, Rotherham United, Chesterfield, Rotherham, Wigan A, Ipswich T, Bury (1990-2010).* Joined United as an apprentice and progressed into the professional ranks for a season. He had loan spells at Oldham and Macclesfield before being handed a free transfer by Sir Alex Ferguson. He has been at Wigan Athletic for the last five years.

POOLE, David

Appearances: 0 Goals: 0 (2003-2005)
Career: *Manchester United, Yeovil Town, Stockport County, Darlington, Stockport County (2003-2010).* Came through the ranks at Old Trafford but never made it into the first team squad. Was allowed to join Yeovil on a free transfer after impressing during a trial game. Is now in his second spell with Stockport County.

POOLE, Terry

Appearances: 0 Goals: 0 (1967-1968)
Career: *Manchester United, Huddersfield Town, Bolton Wanderers, Sheffield United (1967-1981).* He only spent one season at Old Trafford but because of Alex Stepney only missing one game, which Jimmy Rimmer stood in as his deputy, he was allowed to move on to Huddersfield Town where he spent almost a decade. He became manager of a Cash & Carry video wholesaler near Chesterfield, the town of his birth, and lives in Yorkshire.

PORTER, Billy

Appearances: 65 Goals: 0 (1934-1938)
Career: *Oldham Athletic, Manchester United (1926-1938).* Took over the left full-back role from Welsh international Tom Jones, and was an ever present in the 1936 Second Division

Championship winning side. He captained United for most of the War Years before moving on to Hyde United as player manager. Worked at Metro-Vickers during the Second World War, he collapsed and died at Ashton-under-Lyne in April 1946. His friend and Munich victim, Bert Whalley, was with him at the time. He was 40.

PRUNIER, William

Appearances: 2 Goals: 0 (1995-1996)
Career: *Manchester United (1995-1996).* Joined on trial after buying out his Bordeaux contract to link up again with Eric Cantona. Was drafted into first team action with Steve Bruce, Gary Pallister and David May, all injured and made his debut against QPR in December 1995. Then played against Spurs a couple of days later. He was offered an extended trial but opted to move to FC Copenhagen. He joined the coaching staff at AS Cannes but is now in charge of a club in Cugnaux, a suburb of Toulouse.

PUGH, Danny

Appearances: 7 Goals: 0 (2000-2004.)
Career: *Manchester United, Leeds United, Preston, Stoke City (2000-2010).* A midfielder hailing from Cheadle Hulme, Stockport, he made his way through the ranks at Old Trafford making his debut against Maccabi Haifa in the Champions League in September 2002. But after failing to hold down a regular first team place, he was exchanged with Leeds United for Alan Smith. After spending a season on loan at Stoke, he made a permanent move in 2008.

PUUSTINEN, Jami

Appearances: 0 Goals: 0 (2003-2006)
Career: *Manchester United (2003-2006).* A Finnish striker who was offered a three year deal after a successful trial, but left after never making a first team appearance. Is currently playing for FC Honka in his homeland.

QUIXALL, Albert

Appearances: 183 Goals: 56 (1958-1964) Career: Sheffield Wednesday, Manchester United, Oldham Athletic, Stockport County (1950-1966). Probably remembered for his 'short' shorts and boyish looks as much as for his ability to provide passes with pinpoint accuracy. United smashed the British transfer record by paying the Yorkshire Club £45,000 in the wake of the Munich air crash, when they were in need of some vital experience. He enjoyed some success at Old Trafford, winning the FA Cup in 1963 before leaving 12 months later for Oldham in an £8,500 deal, after a being troubled by injury. A full England international, one time golden boy of English football became a scrap dealer in the Manchester area where he now lives in retirement.

RACHUBKA, Paul

Appearances: 3 Goals: 0 (2000-2002) Career: Manchester United, Oldham Athletic, Charlton Athletic, Burnley, Huddersfield Town, Milton Keynes Dons, Northampton Town, Huddersfield Town, Peterborough United, Blackpool (2000-2010). The American keeper joined United as a youngster in 1997. He had a couple of spells out on loan before Sir Alex Ferguson accepted a £200,000 bid from Charlton Athletic. Joined Blackpool on a free transfer after his deal with Huddersfield expired.

RAMMELL, Andy

Appearances: 0 Goals: 0 (1989-1990) Career: Manchester United, Barnsley, Southend United, Walsall, Wycombe Wanderers, Bristol Rovers (1989-2004). Signed as a 22 year old by United from non-league Atherstone United after impressing United scout Nobby Stiles. The £40,000 fee from the transfer paid for a stand which they named after him. Sadly he never made the grade at Old Trafford and was sold to Barnsley for £100,000 in September 1990. Now works for the Royal Mail.

RANKIN, John

Appearances: 0 Goals:0 (2000-2003) Career: Manchester United (2000-2003). A Scottish midfielder from Bellshill, North Lanarkshire. Joined United as a trainee in 2000 but never played a first team game before being released, and he returned to Scotland and signed for Ross County. Following a spell with Inverness Caledonian Thistle, he joined Hibs in January 2008 for a fee of around £110,000.

RATCLIFFE, Simon

Appearances: 0 Goals: 0 (1985-1987) Career: Manchester United, Norwich City, Brentford, Gillingham (1985-1998). Spent two years in the United youth team before being offered professional terms by Ron Atkinson, but he never made the breakthrough into the first team squad and was allowed to join Norwich City when Sir Alex Ferguson was installed in the Old Trafford hot seat. Spent two years working as the Gills youth development officer, returned to Norfolk in 2000 and joined the prison service. Now works at Norwich Prison.

RAWLINSON, Mark

Appearances: 0 Goals: 0 (1993-1995) Career: Manchester United, Bournemouth, Exeter City, Bournemouth (1993-2001). He had the choice between Bolton, Everton and Manchester United as a youngster and opted for a move to Old Trafford, joining as a trainee in July 1993 and becoming one of the 'Fergie Fledglings'. Was at the club he supported as a boy for two years before being given a free transfer and moving to the South Coast, spending the next five years at Dean Court. Moved back to the north west from London to play for FC United. Is now retired and owns a personal fitness training business.

REDMAN, Billy
Appearances: 38 Goals: 0 (1950-1954)
Career: *Manchester United, Bury (1950-1956)*. Signed as a professional in November 1946 but had to wait almost four years for Sir Matt Busby to give him his debut. John Aston was pressed into action as a forward for the visit of Sheffield Wednesday in October, giving him his long awaited chance. He looked to have become a regular starter in the 1951-1952 season when he started the first 18 games, enough to give him a League winner's medal. But he lost his place to Roger Byrne. In June 1954, he made the short move to Bury to link up with former United team mates, Stan Pearson and Henry Cockburn. An apprentice draughtsman during his early days at United, he returned to the profession, working in Manchester until his retirement. He died in January 1995.

REDWOOD, Hubert
Appearances: 96 Goals: 4 (1935-1940)
Career: *Manchester United (1935-1940)*. Made his debut against Spurs in September 1935 but didn't establish himself at right full back until 1936-1937. He helped the club to the Second Division title the next season and was tipped for international honours only for war to be declared soon afterwards. He used to travel from his native St. Helens every day with team mate, George Vose. Served in the army during the war but contracted tuberculosis in October 1943, and died aged only 30.

Photo: Dan Mullen

RICHARDSON, Kieran
Appearances: 81 Goals: 11 (2002-2007)
Career: *Manchester United, WBA, Sunderland (2002-2010)*. Snatched from under the noses of West Ham United, he became a reserve team regular in his first season at United. He made his debut against Olympiacos in the Champions League in October 2002 with his first goal coming against Leicester in the League Cup a month later. Nicknamed 'Lord Snooty' by a fanzine, he wasn't popular with the fans and could never command a regular place in the first team but still managed a Premier League winner's medal in 2006-2007 to go with the FA Youth medal he won in 2003, and the League Cup winner's medal two seasons later. Sunderland boss, Roy Keane, paid £5.5 million for him in July 2007.

RIMMER, Jimmy
Appearances: 46 Goals: 0 (1967-1973)
Career: *Manchester United, Swansea City, Arsenal, Aston Villa, Swansea City, Luton Town (1967-1986)*. Homegrown talent who developed through the junior ranks and was one of the youngsters who won the 1964 FA Youth cup. Although first team appearances were few and far between, as deputy to Alex Stepney, he always proved his worth when called upon. A member of the European Cup winning squad in 1968, he played both games in the semi-finals a year later. It wasn't until Wilf McGuinness was manager that he got a run in the first team, when Stepney was injured for four months. He left permanently in February 1974, after a loan spell at Swansea bought him to the attention of Arsenal. Coached at Swansea, where he had a brief spell as manager, spent several years in China working as a goalkeeping coach now lives and works in Canada.

Jimmy Rimmer
Photo: Bashvaldo

RITCHIE, Andy

Appearances: 42 Goals: 13 (1977-1980) Career: Manchester United, Brighton, Leeds United, Oldham Athletic, Scarborough, Oldham Athletic (1977-1999). A Manchester born striker who was marked down as an outstanding prospect from an early age. He progressed through the ranks into the first team and made his league debut against Everton in December 1977. But had to wait until the 1978-1979 season for another chance and bagged a brace against Derby County in his first appearance. He went on to score 10 goals in his first 17 games, he netted two hat tricks against Leeds United and Spurs but despite this, he was unable to win a regular place in the United starting line. In a complete mystery to United fans, the then manager, Dave Sexton, accepted a £500,000 bid from Brighton & Hove Albion in October 1980 to take him to the South Coast. When he hung up his boot, Ritchie initially moved into coaching with one of his former clubs, Leeds United, and then accepted the role as Assistant Manager to Paul Hart at Barnsley. Went on to manage Oldham Athletic, Barnsley and Huddersfield Town, but since 2008 he has been doing pundit work for BBC Radio Leeds and has also worked as a football consultant.

ROBERTS, Charlie

Appearances: 299 Goals: 23 (1904-1913) Career: Grimsby Town, Manchester United, Oldham Athletic (1903-1919). The £600 United paid for the services of a player with less than a year's experience represented quite a gamble, but it paid off as the quick centre wing half, part of the Roberts, Dick Duckworth and Alec Bell trio, went on to become the inspirational captain of the great United team of the Edwardian era, winning two league titles and a FA Cup. A founding member of the PFA and chairman until 1925, Oldham Athletic paid a record £1,750 but his career was ended during the Great War. He became a wholesale tobacconist, and even created a cigarette "Dunrobel" after the famous half back line he was a part of. He also owned stationery and newsagents' shops in the Manchester area. He died at Manchester Royal Infirmary in August 1939, following a cranial operation after suffering extended dizzy spells.

ROBINS, Mark

Appearances: 69 Goals: 17 (1988-1992) Career: Manchester United, Norwich City, Leicester City, FC Copenhagen, Reading, Manchester City, Walsall, Rotherham United, Bristol City, Sheffield Wednesday, Burton Albion (1986-2005). Shot to fame in 1990 after scoring the FA Cup semi-final replay winner in extra time against Oldham. Then made a sub appearance in the final but two years later, he hadn't progressed into the starting line up as often as he wanted, despite being a potent weapon to have on the bench. His frustration prompted a transfer request then an £800,000 move to Norwich City. Robins originally joined Rotherham United as assistant manager before being appointed manager in 2007. In 2009, he left the club to become the boss of Barnsley.

ROBSON, Bryan

Appearances: 457 Goals: 97 (1981-1994) Career: West Bromwich Albion, Manchester United, Middlesbrough (1974-1995). A true captain, Bryan managed to combine tenacious skill with the ability to motivate others around him. His determination was never more evident than when he had to overcome three broken legs in 1976-1967. To his credit, not only did he recover but he also managed to recapture the form that won him the captaincy of both club and country. Originally from County Durham, 'Robbo' followed his former manager, Ron Atkinson, up the M6 from West Bromwich Albion in 1981, in a deal that also saw the arrival of Remi Moses. The £1.5 million paid was a record at the time and thought to be excessive by some critics. However, by the time Bryan finally left the fold in 1994 to run Middlesbrough, there was no doubt that he had fully justified the investment. Won three FA Cup medals, one League Title and a Cup Winners Cup medal in 1990-1991. Appointed player manager of Middlesbrough in May 1994 and spent seven years in the hot seat, has since managed Bradford, WBA, Sheffield United and since September 2009, the Thailand national team, a role he combines with being a global ambassador for United. Also enjoyed a successful business career with a stake in the Birthday chain of card shops.

Bryan Robson with Helen Southworth MP
Photo: www.labouronline.org/wibs/165679

ROCHE, Lee

Appearances: 3 Goals: 0 (1997-2003) Career: Manchester United, Wrexham, Burnley, Wrexham (1999-2007). Lee joined United as a trainee and turned professional, starting a League Cup match against Arsenal and a Champions League tie with Deportivo la Coruna. His only Premier League appearance came as a sub against Newcastle United at the end of 2003. He was handed a free transfer and was signed by Burnley. Joined non-league Droylsden in 2007.

ROCHE, Paddy

Appearances: 53 Goals: 0 (1973-1982) Career: Manchester United, Brentford, Halifax Town, Chester City (1974-1988). Cost United £15,000 from Irish outfit Shelbourne, and spent his first four seasons at Old Trafford as understudy to Alex Stepney. It wasn't until Dave Sexton took over at United that he enjoyed his first extended run in the first team. But then United struck a deal to sign Jim Blyth from Coventry only for him to fail a medical and Gary Bailey was given his chance and quickly established himself. Roche found himself out of favour once again and was sold to Brentford. Republic of Ireland international, was the Football in the Community Officer based at The Shay. Is now working as a van driver.

ROGERS, Martyn

Appearances: 1 Goals: 0 (1977-1979) Career: Manchester United, Queens Park Rangers (1977-1981). An outstanding record at school boy level could never be translated in the senior game, and he made just one appearance for United standing in for Arthur Albiston in a 4-0 defeat against WBA in October 1977. He was allowed to join former United boss, Tommy Docherty, but even in the capital he struggled to make an impact. After a spell playing for Sydney Olympic, he returned to England but sadly committed suicide in a fume filled hire car in March 1992, in a Ringwood car park, Hampshire, aged just 32.

Photo: A:3KFootball

RONALDO, Cristiano

Appearances: 292 Goals: 118 (2003-2009) Career: Manchester United (2003-2009). Signed from Sporting CP in a £12.24 million deal, he was the first Portuguese player to ever pull on the United shirt.

And his record for years to come will rank alongside the greatest players to have played for the club. By the time he left Old Trafford, had did so with three Premier League titles, FA Cup, League Cup, Champions League and World Club Cup winner's medals. Three times he was voted Sir Matt Busby Player of the Year, and in 2008 was named FIFA World Player and Ballon d'Or winner. He joined a long list of great players: Best, Robson, Cantona and Beckham, to have worn the number 7 shirt. In July 2009 after years of speculation, he signed for Real Madrid in an £80 million deal making him the most expensive player in the history of the game, and is currently the highest paid player in the world.

ROSE, Danny

Appearances: 0 Goals: 0 (2002-2007) Career: Manchester United, Oxford U (2002-2010). Spent five years at Old Trafford progressing through the youth system and into the reserves, who he captained in 2006-2007. He was released at the end of that season. Despite having a trial at Bristol Rovers, he joined Oxford United where he had a spell on loan.

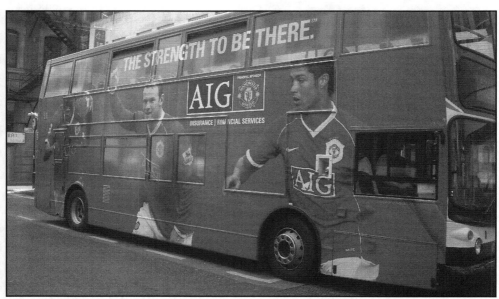

Photo: dullhunk

ROSE, Michael

Appearances: 0 Goals: 0 (2000-2001)
Career: *Manchester United, Chester C,*
Hereford U, Yeovil T, Cheltenham T,
Scunthorpe U, Norwich C, Swindon T
(2000-2010). The Salford born left back
spent a year as a trainee at Old Trafford
before being released and dropping out
of the Football League with Chester. An
England semi-pro international, he joined
Swindon on a free transfer in June 2010.

ROSSI, Guiseppe

Appearances: 14 Goals: 4 (2004-2007)
Career: *Manchester United, Newcastle*
United (2004-2007). The American
born striker moved to Italy with his
father to play in Parma's youth team, but
United bought out his contract when he
was 17. He is best remembered for a
superb goal against Sunderland at the
Stadium of Light. United sold him in July
2007 to Spanish side Villarreal for £6.6
million but included a buy back clause
in the deal.

ROWLEY, Jack

Appearances: 424 Goals: 209 (1937-
1955) Career: *Wolves, Bournemouth,*
Manchester United, Plymouth A (1935-
1956). Signed by United for £3,000, he
helped the club to promotion in his first
season but it was after the World War
Two that he really made his name,
becoming one of the top centre
forwards of the time. He was a regular
in the United side which finished
runners up in four seasons out of five,
and scored twice in the 1948 FA Cup
Final win over Blackpool. Dubbed the
Gunner, mainly because of his explosive
shooting, he scored 30 goals as United
marched to the title in 1951-1952. He
only left United to take charge of
Plymouth Argyle. Coached Ajax in
Holland and managed Plymouth,
Wrexham, Bradford and Oldham. Ran a
newsagents and then a post office
before retiring to Shaw, Oldham, where
he died in June 1998, aged 77.

RUSSELL, Martin

Appearances: 0 Clubs: 0 (1984-1987)
Career: *Manchester United,*
Birmingham C, Norwich C, Leicester C,
Scarborough, Middlesbro (1984-1991).
Joined United from school but couldn't
break into the first team squad at Old
Trafford and was allowed to leave Old
Trafford to move to Leicester. Is
currently employed as first team
manager and Academy director at UCD.
He also coaches in schools.

RYAN, David

Career: *Manchester United, Port Vale,*
Southport (1974-1976). The
Manchester born goalkeeper joined
United as an apprentice in 1974, and
made his league debut on loan to Port
Vale. After returning to Old Trafford, he
failed to make a first team appearance
and was released. He spent a season at
Southport before dropping out of the
league. Spent 11 successful years at
Northwich Victoria. Is now the landlord
of The Witch in Lindfield, Lancashire.

Photo: Leslie Millman

RYAN, Jimmy

*Appearances: 27 Goals: 4 (1965-1970)
Career: Manchester United, Luton Town
(1965-1976).* A winger who had
everything needed to reach the top of
the game, but at Old Trafford he found
his chances limited by George Best,
John Connelly and John Aston. It wasn't
until he moved to Luton, that his career
began to take off. He later played for
Dallas Tornados where he was a team
mate of Alex Stepney once again. Is
now the director of United's Youth
Academy. Was briefly first team coach
and also took charge of the reserves, a
job that he had done at Luton.

SADLER, Adam

*Appearances: 0 Goals: 0 (1996-1998)
Career: Manchester United (1996-
1998).* Spent two years at Old Trafford,
before spending a further season at
Barnsley and dropping out of the full-
time game. Worked for Newcastle
United and Norwich City, is now head of
youth development at Plymouth Argyle.

SADLER, David

*Appearances: 335 Goals: 27 (1963-
1974) Career: Manchester United,
Preston (1963-1976).* Plucked from
non-league Maidstone, he broke into
United's first team at 17 in August 1963.

Photo: *Sporting Memorabilia*

The same season he was an FA Youth
Cup Final scoring a hat trick against
Swindon in the final. But it wasn't until
he was converted to defence that his
career really took off. He was part of
the team that won the 1966-1967 title
and the 1968 European Cup. He ended
his career with Preston, managed by his
former United team mate Bobby
Charlton. An England international,
spent many years as a branch manager
for a building society in Hale, returning
to the profession he took up before
becoming a footballer. Then ran his
own corporate hospitality company in
Manchester and acts as secretary to the
ex-United Players' Association.

Photo: *nicksarebi*

SAHA, Luis

*Appearances:120 Goals: 42 (2004-
2008) Career: Newcastle U, Fulham,
Manchester United, Everton (1999-
2010).* The French striker arrived at
Old Trafford for £12.8 million in January
2004, after scoring 15 goals in the first
half of the 2003-2004 season. He
started his United contract on fire with 7
goals in his first 10 starts. But he never
fulfilled his potential after a string of
niggling injuries. He still managed to
bag two Premier League titles, a League
Cup and a Champions League winner's
medals by the time he joined Everton
in the summer of 2008.

SARTORI, Carlos

Appearances: 56 Goals: 6 (1968-1973)
Career: *Manchester United (1968-1973).*
The first Italian to play for United after his family moved to Collyhurst when he was a youngster, he signed as a professional on his 17th birthday but he had to wait three years for his chance in the first team. He struggled to hold down a regular first team place and was mainly a reserve. He eventually returned to Italy in January 1973 to join Bologna in a £50,000 deal. Ran a successful knife sharpening business, which has brought him the comfort of three homes in Italy and a comfortable house on the outskirts of Rochdale.

Photo: Ned Trifle

SAVAGE, Robbie

Appearances: 0 Appearances: 0 (1991-1994) Career: *Manchester United, Crewe Alexandra, Leicester City, Birmingham City, Blackburn Rovers, Derby County, Brighton (1993-2010).*
Savage was signed by United as a striker and was part of the 1992 FA Youth Cup winning side. After spending two years as a trainee, he was given a one year professional deal but couldn't make the breakthrough into the first team squad. Was released to join Crewe Alexandra. Joined Derby in 2008, and works as a media pundit for the BBC.

SAVAGE, Robert

Appearances: 5 Goals: 0 (1937-1938)
Career: *Lincoln City, Liverpool, Manchester United, Wrexham (1928-1940).* Signed by United as half back cover and was given a run of games as deputy for James Brown, Coached in Holland and managed South Liverpool post war , before running the Primrose Hotel in Wallasey until his death in January 1964, aged 51.

Photo: Sporting Memorabilia

SCANLON, Albert

Appearances: 127 Goals: 35 (1954-1961) Career: *Manchester United, Newcastle U, Lincoln C, Mansfield T (1954-1966).* The nephew of former United winger Charlie Mitten, competed for a first team place with David Pegg prior to Munich, when he suffered head and leg injuries. Luckily he went on to make a full recovery. He became a regular for two seasons, helping United to finish runners up in 1958-1959 when he scored 16 goals. Later lived in Salford, worked on the docks for 16 years then finally as a security guard at a Colgate Palmolive plant near Old Trafford. He was buried in the same Weaste Cemetery as Eddie Colman, after his death in December 2009, aged 74.

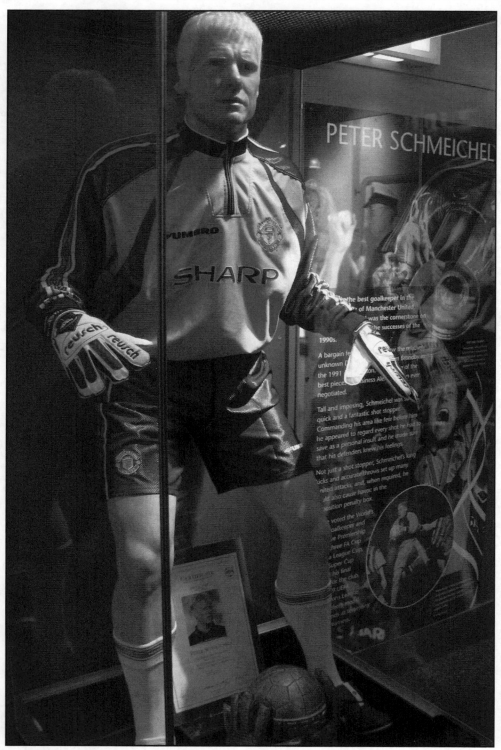

Photo: Steve Montgomery

SCHMEICHEL, Peter

Appearances: 398 Goals: 1 (1991-1999)
Career: Manchester United, Aston Villa,
Manchester City (1981-2003). The
'Great Dane' has proved to be an
inspirational last line of defence ever
since his signing from Danish club
Brondby in 1991, for what has proved to
be a giveaway fee by today's standards
of only £500,000. While his colleagues
may grab the glory of match winning
goals, it has often only been possible
because 6ft 4in Peter has done such a
magnificent job at the other end. By the
time he left Old Trafford, he had won five
Premier League titles, three FA Cups,
four Charity Shields, a League Cup,
Super Cup and a Champions League.
He ended his United career with the
treble before joining Sporting Lisbon.
Since retirement, Schmeichel has
worked as television football pundit for
the BBC in England and TV3+ in
Denmark. He owned his childhood side
Hvidovre IF for several years before
withdrawing himself. He has also taken
part in charity football matches such as
Soccer Aid, and has appeared in reality
television shows such as "Strictly Come
Dancing". In his native Denmark, he has
also become a TV show presenter of
quiz show "1 mod 100" and the
european version of the Discovery
Channel show "Dirty Jobs".

SCOTT, Jackie

Appearances: 3 Goals: 0 (1952-1956.)
Career: Manchester United, Grimsby
Town, York City (1952-1964). Scott was
the first player from Northern Ireland to
be sent to Old Trafford by scout Bob
Bishop. He made his first team debut in
December 1952 against Wolves, but with
chances to impress limited, he moved to
Grimsby who were managed by his
former United colleague, Allenby
Chilton. The Northern Ireland
international lost his life aged only 44 in
tragic circumstances in June 1978, after
an accident on the Manchester building
site where he was employed.

SEALEY, Les

Appearances: 33 Goals: 0 (1990-1991 &
1993-1994) Career: Coventry City,
Luton Town, Plymouth Argyle,
Manchester United, Aston Villa,
Birmingham City, Blackpool, West Ham
United, Leyton Orient, Bury (1976-2000).
Joined United initially on loan and ended
up playing in the 1990 FA Cup Final
replay win over Crystal Palace, after a
horror show by Jim Leighton. Signed
permanently and became a cult hero
after playing in the Cup Winner's Cup
Final victory over Barcelona, he left for
Aston Villa after only being offered a one
year deal but rejoined United on a free
transfer to act as understudy to Peter
Schmeichel. He played in the League
Cup Final defeat to Aston Villa before
being given a free transfer and moving
to Blackpool. Sealey was appointed
player-goalkeeper coach of West Ham
United in 1999. He died of a heart
attack on the 19th August 2001, aged 43.

SETTERS, Maurice

Appearances: 194 Goals: 14 (1960-
1964) Career: Exeter City, WBA,
Manchester United, Stoke C, Coventry
City, Charlton Athletic (1953-1969). A
real battler who made the switch from
West Brom for £30,000 in 1960. He was a
FA Cup winner in 1963 and enjoyed four
years in a red shirt before moving on to
Stoke in November 1964, in a £30,000
deal. When it became clear that he
wasn't going to dislodge Nobby Stiles
from the first team, and he wanted to
play more regular first team football, at
the end of the season that he left, United
won the League Championship. Went
into management with Doncaster
Rovers, then had stops at Sheffield
Wednesday (coach), Rotherham United
(assistant manager), Newcastle United
(chief Scout) and was assistant manager
of the Republic of Ireland national team
for ten years. Lives in retirement in
Tichill, Doncaster.

Photo: Antonia Sterland

SHARPE, Lee

Appearances: 263 Goals: 37 (1988-1997) Career: Torquay United, Manchester United, Leeds United, Bradford City, Portsmouth, Exeter City (1988-2002). Shrewdly identified as a star of the future, Alex Ferguson gave Torquay United £200,000 for the teenager in 1988. Seven years later, his investment was repaid but not necessarily as he may have hoped. Despite the fact that Leeds happily parted with £4.5 million to take Lee to Yorkshire in 1996, many supporters would have preferred that early eye-catching performances, that led to his original rise to full England international, had continued in a red shirt. A former PFA Young Player of the Year, he won two FA Cup winner's medals and a Cup Winners Cup medal, as well as a league Championship title. Since retirement, Sharpe has appeared as a television football pundit for the BBC, as well as appearing on reality TV shows such as "Celebrity Love Island", "Celebrity Wrestling" and "Dancing on Ice". He has also appeared in "Coronation Street", has released his autobiography and is now an official dinner speaker for Manchester United.

SHAWCROSS, Ryan

Appearances: 2 Goals: 0 (2006-2008) Career: Manchester United, Stoke City (2006-2010). He made steady progress through the youth teams and reserves before being handed his debut against Crewe in the League Cup in October 2006. He was unable to break into the first team squad and was sold to Stoke, for an initial £1 million.

SHERINGHAM, Teddy

Appearances: 153 Goals: 46 (1997-2001) Career: Millwall, Aldershot T, Notts F, Tottenham H, Manchester United, Portsmouth, West Ham U, Colchester U(1983-2008). Bought for £3.5 million from Spurs in 1997 to replace Eric Cantona. Then at the age of 33, he was part of their treble winning side despite having to play second fiddle to Andy Cole and Dwight Yorke for much of the campaign. He scored in the FA Cup Final and Champions League Finals. In 1999-2000, he finished up as top scorer as United retained their title earning him Player of the Year awards from the PFA and Football Writers. He stayed at Old Trafford for a fourth and final season before returning to Spurs. Sheringham has appeared as a television football pundit since retirement but has mainly and notably become a professional poker player.

SIDEBOTTOM, Arnie

Appearances: 20 Goals: 0 (1972-1975)
Career: *Manchester United,*
Huddersfield Town, Halifax Town (1972-1979). A fast bowler with Yorkshire and England, he was first handed his chance in the first team against Sheffield United in March 1973, as deputy for Steve James. But it wasn't until Jim Holton broke his leg in the 1974-1975 promotion winning season, when he played 12 games, that he was given a run of games in the first team. After winning promotion, he departed Old Trafford in January 1976 to join fourth division Huddersfield Town. His son, Ryan, has followed in his footsteps into the England cricket team, while he now coaches football and cricket at Woodhouse Grove School in West Yorkshire.

SILCOCK, John

Appearances: 449 Goals: 2 (1919-1934)
Career: *Manchester United, Oldham Athletic (1917-1935).* Spotted by the then United manager, John Robson, after he went to watch another player and he impressed enough to be asked to join United's amateur ranks, before signing professional. Over the next 15 seasons, he was a first team regular forming a dominant partnership with Charlie Moor. Despite playing almost 450 games at Old Trafford, he didn't win any medals but did at least play three times for England before leaving for Oldham Athletic. Worked as a miner before joining United, he later became a licensee in the Manchester area. He died in June 1966, aged 68.

SILVESTRE, Mikaël

Appearances: 361 Goals: 10 (1999-2008) Career: *Manchester United, Arsenal (1999-2010).* French defender, joined United from Inter Milan for £4 million and spent the next nine seasons in the United first team squad.

Mikael Silvestre
Photo: Ronnie Macdonald

He could play at either left back or in the middle of the back four, forming a number of partnerships that were key to the success enjoyed by the club. During his time at Old Trafford, he won four Premier League titles, one FA Cup, one League Cup, two FA Charity Shields and a Champions League title. He looked set for a move across Manchester in 2008 to joined City, but changed his mind at the last minute and moved to Arsenal instead. After being released by The Gunners in the summer of 2010, he joined Werder Bremen.

SIMPSON, Danny

Appearances: 8 Goals: 0 (2006-2010)
Career: *Manchester United, Sunderland, Ipswich T, Blackburn R, Newcastle U (2006-2010).* A Salford born defender who was a product of United's youth system, he was promoted into the reserves in 2005 and signed his first professional contract in 2006. His debut came against Coventry in the League Cup in September 2007, with his Premier League coming against Wigan a month later. He had spells out on loan, the final one coming at Newcastle, and he completed a £750,000 permanent move to St. James Park.

SIVEBAEK, Johnny

Appearances: 34 Goals: 1 (1985-1987)
Career: *Manchester United (1985-
1987)*. Arrived at Old Trafford for
£285,000 in February 1986 from Vejle, in
the middle of a programme of heavy
investment, after failing his first medical
with the club. He took time to settle into
the English game and it wasn't until the
start of the 1986-1987 season that
United started to really see what the
Danish international was capable of
achieving. An attacking minded right
back, he lost his place under Sir Alex
Ferguson who preferred Mike Duxbury,
and he departed for St. Etienne in
France for £220,000. Is living in his
native Vejle and works as a football
agent for First Artist Scandinavia.

SLOAN, Paddy

Appearances: 0 Goals: 0 (1937-1938)
Career: *Manchester United, Tranmere
Rovers, Arsenal, Sheffield United,
Norwich City, Peterborough United
(1937-1954)*. Signed for United from
Glenavon but never played a first team
game and was sold to Tranmere for
£500. He returned to Old Trafford
during the war and played both legs of
the League North Cup Final against
Bolton Wanderers. After the war, he
played for AC Milan among a number of
other Italian clubs. Emigrated to
Australia to coach South Melbourne
Hallas and then Juventus, he later
coached in Turkey and became
chairman of the National Soccer
Coaches Association. He died in
January 1993, aged 72.

Photo: edwin.11

SLOAN, Tom

Appearances: 12 Goals: 0 (1978-1982)
Career: *Manchester United, Chester
City (1978-1983)*. Signed for £20,000 in
the summer of 1978 from right under
the noses of Spurs, but he had to wait
until September the same year for his
league debut in place of Lou Macari, in
a 2-0 win over Ipswich Town. But he
was unable to hold down a regular in
the first team and was allowed to move
onto Chester City. Returned to his
native Ballymena to work as a self-
employed plasterer.

SMITH, Alan

Appearances: 93 Goals: 12 (2004-2007)
Career: *Leeds United, Manchester
United, Newcastle United (1998-2010)*.
Arrived at Old Trafford for £7 million in
August 2004 with a big reputation after
a stunning start to his career at Leeds.
He scored on his debut in the Charity
but that proved to be one of a few high
points of his time at Old Trafford. Hit by
a string of injuries in his first season at
United, he broke his leg early into his
second campaign. After being out of
action for almost 12 months, he came
back in 2006-2007 but couldn't hold
down a regular place, but did win a
Premier League winner's medal.
Newcastle United made a successful £6
million move for Smith in August 2007.

SMITH, Bobby

Appearances: 0 Goals: 0 (1961-1965)
Career: *Manchester United, Scunthorpe
United, Grimsby Town, Brighton,
Chester City, Hartlepool United, Bur.
(1961-1973)*. Hailing from Prestbury, he
joined United in 1961 making over 250
reserve team appearances without ever
playing for the first team, and eventually
leaving for Scunthorpe. Managed Bury,
Port Vale, Swindon, Newport, Swansea
then on to the coaching staff of Sheffield
Wednesday until 1999. Also had spells
at Hereford and Cardiff City.

SOLSKJAER, Ole Gunnar

Appearances: 366 Goals: 126 (1996-2007) Career: Manchester United (1996-2007). Fast and skillful Norwegian international with an eye for goal. Solskjaer was acquired from Molde (Norway) in July 1996 for a fee of £1.5 million and is best remembered for scoring the last minute injury time winner against Bayern Munich in the 1999 Champions League Final to complete the treble. Often used as a Super Sub, he did briefly partner Ruud van Nistelrooy in front and played on the right wing for a spell when David Beckham was injured. He was troubled with knee injuries and was eventually forced to announce his retirement from the game. He holds the United record for the most goals by a substitute 28. In November 2007, Solskjaer was awarded with First Class of the Royal Norwegian Order of St. Olav by King Harald V of Norway, the Norwegian equivalent of knighthood. He was presented with the award in a ceremony on the 25 October 2008, in his hometown of Kristiansund. Solskjaer is the youngest ever recipient of the knighthood, usually bestowed upon notable members of society in their later years. Since 2008, he has been the reserve team manager of Manchester United.

SPECTOR, Jonathan

Appearances: 8 Goals: 0 (2003-2006) Career: Manchester United, Charlton Athletic, West Ham United (2003-2010). An American defender who was spotted by scout, Jimmy Ryan, playing in the Milk Cup in 2003, and he was signed from Chicago Fire Premier. He made his debut in the Charity Shield a year later but was sold to West Ham in June 2006 for £500,000, after failing to hold down a regular first team place. His grandfather, Art Spector, was the first player signed by the Boston Celtics in 1946.

SPOONER, Nicky

Appearances: 0 Goals: 0 (1987-1989) Career: Manchester United, Bolton Wanderers, Oldham Athletic, Chester City (1987-2000). Spent two years at Old Trafford as a trainee but never got to play a game for the first team before he was handed a free transfer and allowed to join Bolton Wanderers. Is now back at Bolton, where he is assistant Academy coach and development manager.

STACEY, George

Appearances: 267 Goals: 9 (1907-1919) Career: Barnsley, Manchester United (1905-1919). A man of few words, nicknamed 'Silent Stacey' by his team mates, he joined United for £200 as understudy to Herbert Burgess. A powerful back, he became a regular and won two League titles with an FA Cup win sandwiched in between. He lacked the pace to become an international, but continued to play until the Great War and was released in 1919. He opened his own small business in Barnsley before returning to his former professional as a coal miner.

STAFFORD, Harry

Appearances: 200 Goals: 0 (1896-1903) Career: Crewe A, Newton Heath, Manchester United, Crewe Alexandra (1890-1903). He was United's first ever captain, having continued in the role he held when Newton Heath ran into financial problems. Legend has it that it was Stafford's dog 'Major' that brought Stafford and John Henry Davies together, leading to Davies, a wealthy brewery owner, buying the club and whipping the debt away while Stafford became groundsman and a director of the club when he retired. He ran a pub in Wrexham before emigrating to Australia but he ended up living in Canada, where he owned a large hotel. His son, Harry Jnr, died in December 1988, aged 87, a victim of killer GP Harold Shipman.

Photo: Flovries

STAM, Jaap

Appearances: 127 Goals: 1 (1998-2002)
Career: *Manchester United (1998-2001)*. He only spent three seasons at Old Trafford after he became the most expensive Dutch player in history, when he moved from PSV Eindhoven for £10.6 million. During his time with the club, United won three Premier League titles, one FA Cup, an Intercontinental Cup and a Champions League crown. He fell out with Sir Alex Ferguson after comments he made about him and the club in his autobiography and he was sold to Italian outfit Lazio for £16.5m. Is now working for United as their South American scout and is on the coaching staff of FC Zwolle, in his native Holland.

STAPLETON, Frank

Appearances: 288 Goals: 78 (1981-1987) Career: Arsenal, Manchester United, Derby C, Blackburn R, Aldershot, Huddersfield T, Bradford C, Brighton (1974-1994). Republic of Ireland international and great header of the ball who was acquired from Arsenal for a tribunal set £900,000 in August 1981, almost a decade after he had an unsuccessful trial at Old Trafford.

He was bought to succeed Joe Jordan. He became a Fans' Favourite and helped the club to win two FA Cups in 1983 and 1985. He scored against Brighton and became the first player to score for different clubs in Wembley Finals. Soon after Brian McClair arrived at the club, he moved to Ajax on the recommendation of former team mate, Arnold Muhren. Managed at Bradford City, was QPR reserve team coach, then managed New England in the MLS. Was also a specialist coach at Bolton and is now a media pundit and after dinner speaker, living in Manchester.

STEELE, Luke

Appearances: 0 Goals: 0 (2002-2006)
Career: *Peterborough United, Manchester United, Coventry City, West Bromwich Albion, Coventry City, Barnsley (2001-2010)*. England under-18 keeper, started out at his local club Peterborough. After Roy Carroll and Ricardo left Old Trafford, £500,000 was paid to Posh to bring him to Old Trafford permanently after a loan spell. A member of the 2002-2003 Youth Cup winning side, he was third choice but never played a first team game before moving to West Brom. Has been at Barnsley since 2008.

Frank Stapleton

Photo: *Sporting Memorabilia*

STEPNEY, Alex

Appearances: 539 Goals: 2 (1966-1979)
Career: *Millwall, Chelsea, Manchester United (1963-1979)*. Signed for a record transfer fee of £55,000 from Chelsea after only playing one game in three months for the London side, he soon established himself as regular first choice at Old Trafford and collected a League Championship winner's medal at the end of his first season. He won a European Cup winner's medal in 1968, a week after playing his only game for England. He was briefly challenged for his place in the team by Jimmy Rimmer and Paddy Roche, he won a second Division Championship medal and was then a FA Cup winner in 1977. He even managed to score two goals, both in 1973. He ran a van hire business in Rochdale, also ran a pub, worked in a car body repair shop, was commercial manager at Rochdale FC and coached the goalkeepers at Man City. Was a radio chat show host in Manchester. Is now an after dinner speaker and works on MUTV.

STEWARD, Alf

Appearances: 326 Goals: 0 (1920-1932)
Career: *Manchester United (1920-1932)*.
He wrote to United asking for a trial after a contract dispute with Stalybridge Celtic, and ironically made his debut for United reserves against his former club. He was seen as a safe pair of hands and became a first team regular when he replaced Jack Mew. He was an ever present in United's 1924-1925 promotion winning side but won no further honours because of a lean period in the club's history. He had two benefits and left Old Trafford after 12 years to manage Manchester North End. He managed Torquay United for two years before the Second World War and then moved to the Birmingham area to work on munitions, and later became group secretary of the BSA Recreation Centre in the city.

STEWART, Michael

Appearances: 14 Goals: 0 (1998-2005)
Career: *Manchester United, Nottingham Forest (1998-2005)*. A highly rated youngster who was signed by United from under the noses of Rangers. He went on to make his debut against Watford in 2000, but he couldn't hold down a regular first team. A move to Rangers fell through before he moved to Hibs after SAF told him he had no future at the club. Has played for both Edinburgh clubs, left Hearts in the summer and now plays for Turkish outfit Genclerbirligi.

Photo: *toksuede*

Photo: www.gilesgphotography.co.uk

STILES, Nobby

Appearances: 3395 Goals: 19 (1960-1971) Career: Manchester United, Middlesbrough, Preston (1960-1974). Is best remembered for his jig after England's famous 1966 World Cup victory, a tough aggressive half back but there was much more to him than a hard man image. He was a vital part of Sir Matt Busby's team that won two championship medals, and the European Cup Winners medal in 1968 after overcoming the disappointment of missing the 1963 FA Cup Final against Leicester City. To have huge influence in the success that the club enjoyed, he played in contact lenses after Busby sent him to have his eyes tested to improve his game after too many poor challenges. He secured his place as a true United legend before leaving for Middlesbrough in a £20,000 deal. He managed WBA and was a co-director of United's School of Excellence. Is now an after dinner speaker. His son, John, played for Leeds.

STOREY-MOORE, Ian

Appearances: 43 Goals: 12 (1971-1973) Career: Nottingham Forest, Manchester United (1963-1973). Moved to United for £200,000 in March 1972, after an abortive move to Derby County where Brian Clough paraded him on the pitch as a new signing. One of the best goal scoring wingers of his day, he scored on his debut against Huddersfield Town in March 1972 to give United their first victory for three months. He then scored in his next two games but injuries took their toll and he was forced to retire on medical advice, 18 months after arriving at Old Trafford. Capped by England, he became a successful businessman in Nottingham where he was a publican and owned a bookmakers, but is now chief scout at Aston Villa having previously had same role at the City Ground.

STRACHAN, Gordon

Appearances: 201 Goals: 38 (1984-1989) Career: Manchester United, Leeds United, Coventry City (1984-1997). A real Fans' Favourite, the little red haired Scotsman was ironically sold to United by his future manager, Alex Ferguson, for £600,000 as a replacement for Ray Wilkins. Together they had previously contributed to Aberdeen's period of domination north of the border. Once at Old Trafford, they both more than made their mark. Strachan scored 15 goals in his first season which also produced an FA Cup winner's medal, and he produced a sackful of memorable displays in the following years until his surprise departure for Leeds United in March 1989, in a £300,000 deal. The Scottish international managed Coventry and Southampton before taking Celtic to three league titles in the four years he was in charge. Has been Middlesbrough's boss since October 2009 and worked as a media pundit when in between jobs.

SWITZER, George

Appearances: 0 Goals: 0 (1992-1993)
Career: *Manchester United, Darlington (1992-1994).* A FA Youth Cup winner in 1992 alongside David Beckham, Gary Neville, Ryan Giggs and Paul Scholes. He spent a year at Old Trafford as a professional but was released because he was considered too small to play at left back. In all, he spent a decade at the club and moved to Darlington on a free transfer. After dropping into the non-league game, he has worked as an optical technician for Dolland & Aitchison at their factory in Salford and driving a van for a Manchester courier firm.

TAIBI, Massimo

Appearances: 4 Goals: 0 (1999-2000)
Career: *Manchester United (1999-2000).* Signed for £4.4 million to compete with Mark Bosnich and Raimond van der Gouw for the number one goalkeeping spot at Old Trafford, he only played four games but they were eventful. A mistake on his debut allowed Liverpool's Sami Hyypia to score, is best remembered for a gaffe which allowed a Matt le Tissier shot under his body, while a 5-0 defeat to Chelsea was one of United's heaviest for 25 years. He was later allowed to return to Italy with Reggina. Lends a hand helping to coach at his home town team of Palermo.

TAPKEN, Norman

Appearances: 16 Goals: 0 (1938-1939)
Career: *Newcastle United, Manchester United, Darlington (1933-1948).* United paid £850 to sign him from Newcastle on Christmas Eve 1938, in the last season before the Second World War. Made his debut against Leicester City at Old Trafford two days later. He enjoyed an 11 game run in the first team before sharing the goalkeeping duties with John Breedon and Tommy Breen.

The outbreak of war spelt the end of his Old Trafford career. He didn't even guest for the club during hostilities. After returning from Ireland where he ended his career, he was assistant trainer at Stoke City. He then became a publican in Newcastle-under-Lyme until retiring. Died in June 1996.

TATE, Alan

Appearances: 0 Goals: 0 (2000-2004)
Career: *Manchester United, Swansea City (2000-2010).* Started his United career as a trainee before going on to captain the reserves. After two loan spells, was allowed to permanently join Swansea City.

TAYLOR, Ernie

Appearances: 30 Goals: 4 (1957-1959)
Career: *Newcastle United, Blackpool, Manchester United, Sunderland (1942-1961).* The first emergency signing by Jimmy Murphy when he had to rebuild following the Munich air crash, and he proved to be a superb £8,000 signing. In his ten months at the club. He helped bring some stability and the club reached a FA Cup Final. In December 1958, he was sold to Sunderland for £7,000 after losing his place to United's then record signing Albert Quixall. He emigrated to New Zealand where he coached New Brighton in Christchurch, before returning to England to work for Vauxhall Motors in Hooten. Was also adviser to Heswell FC in the Cheshire League. He died on Birkenhead in April 1985, aged 59.

TAYLOR, Kris

Appearances: 0 Goals: 0 (2001-2003)
Career: *Manchester United, Walsall, Burton Albion, Port Vale (2001-2010).* Signed for £200,000 from Wolves Academy. After only a handful of reserve team appearance and without breaking into the first team, he was allowed to leave for Walsall. He joined Port Vale in 2009 after a successful trial.

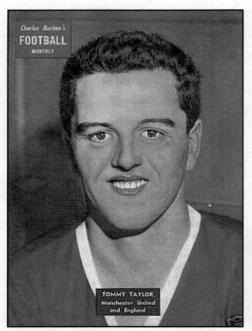

Photo: David Mullen

TAYLOR, Tommy

Appearances: 191 Goals: 131 (1953-1958) Career: Barnsley, Manchester United (1949-1958). One of the finest centre forwards to have set foot on the hallowed turf, Matt Busby justifiably paid £29,999 (he reportedly gave a pound to the tea lady to avoid Tommy having to carry the burden of a £30,000 price tag). In the process, the existing transfer record was broken to acquire the Yorkshireman's sensational scoring skills to replace the legendary Jack Rowley. He started his United career with 7 goals in 8 games, he won League Championship medals in 1956 and 1957, and he also scored in the 1957 FA Cup final defeat against Aston Villa. United turned down a world record bid of £65,000 from Inter Milan for him the year before his death. At international level he scored 16 goals in only 18 England appearances. He was sadly only 26 when he lost his life on the runway at Munich. He is buried at Monk Bretton Cemetery in his home town, Barnsley.

TEATHER, Paul

Appearances: 0 Goals: 0 (1994-2001) Career: Manchester United, Bournemouth (1994-2001). Joined United after leaving school in 1994, but he never played a first team game and was released, dropping into non-league football before having to retire through injury. Got a physiotherapy degree from the University of Salford,then worked at both Sheffield clubs and now works as a musculoskeletal specialist for a private practice.

Photo: toksuede

TEVEZ, Carlos.

Appearances: 63 Goals: 19 (2007-2009) Career: West Ham, Manchester United Manchester City (2001-date). An Argentinian of undoubted brilliance on his day, but controversy seems to have have followed him around. Admittedly, not all of it has been of his own making, however after two years at Old Trafford he decided that he no longer wanted to play for the club. It had been reported that Sir Alex was prepared to meet the £25m fee required to make his signing permanent and had offered the player a lucrative five year deal. tevez signed for Manchester City on 14th July 2009.

THOMAS, Geoff

Appearances: 0 Goals: 0 (1973)
Career: *Swansea City, Manchester United (1966-1975)*. A former Wales under-23, he served Swansea for over a decade. Arrived at Old Trafford in December 1973 on loan, on the recommendation of Harry Gregg, but he never played a first team game and returned to South Wales. After retiring, he became a milkman in the Mumbles, Swansea, where he still lives.

THOMAS, Mickey

Appearances: 110 Goals: 15 (1978-1981) Career: *Wrexham, Manchester United, Everton, Brighton, Stoke C, Chelsea, WBA, Derby C, Shrewsbury T, Leeds United, Stoke City, Wrexham (1971-1991)*. Welsh international winger who arrived in Manchester from Wrexham for a fee of £300,000, under the reign of Dave Sexton. He appeared in a FA Cup Final against Arsenal at the end of his first season at the club. He might have lacked skill and shooting power but his work rate was beyond doubt, he became a better all round player under Sexton. However, he moved to Everton in exchange for John Gidman just weeks after the arrival of Ron Atkinson as manager in the summer of 1981. Was a youth coach at Wrexham until doing a stretch at Her Majesty's pleasure for his part in a counterfeit money scam. Is now a radio summariser and an after dinner speaker.

THORNLEY, Ben

Appearances: 14 Goals: 0 (1993-1998)
Career: *Manchester United, Stockport County, Huddersfield Town, Blackpool, Bury, Halifax (1993-2004)*. Another member of United's 1992 FA Youth Cup winning squad. Rated highly by SAF but just as it seemed set he was going to make it all the way to the top, he suffered a serious knee injury after a horror tackle in a reserve game and spent a year on the sidelines. He was eventually released on a free transfer in May 1998. Dropped into non-league football and was last heard to be driving a cab.

Mickey Thomas (middle) with fellow ex-pros.
Photo: United Nights

THORRINGTON, John

Appearances: 0 Goals: 0 (1997-1999)
Career: *Manchester United, Huddersfield Town, Grimsby Town (1997-2004)*. South African born midfielder who spent two years at Old Trafford playing for the youth team. He moved to Germany and joined Bayer Leverkusen without making a first team appearance. Moved to the States in 2005 to play for Chicago Fire.

TIERNEY, Paul

Appearances: 1 Goals: 0 (2000-2005)
Career: *Manchester United, Crewe, Colchester, Bradford, Blackpool, Stockport County (2000-2008)*. Only made one appearance in the League Cup against WBA in December 2003, but after failing to make an impact on the first team squad, he was handed a free transfer in June 2005. The Republic of Ireland international had spells at a number of clubs in England and Scotland. Played for Altrincham until 2010.

TIMM, Mads

Appearances: 1 Goals: 0 (2002-2006)
Career: *Manchester United, Walsall (2002-2006)*. Signed a professional deal in 2002 and won the FA Youth Cup 12 months later, but he only made one first team appearance in the Champions League. In 2005, he was sentenced to 12 months in a young offenders institution for dangerous driving but couldn't break into the first team squad and returned home to Denmark to join his home town club. Odense. Announced he was retiring in 2009 after a season with Lyngby, aged 24.

TOMLINSON, Graeme

Appearances: 2 Goals: 0 (1994-1998)
Career: *Bradford City, Manchester United, Luton Town, AFC Bournemouth, Millwall, Macclesfield Town, Exeter CitY (1993-2002)*. Signed for £500,000 from Bradford City, he only made two appearances as a sub before being sent out on loan to Luton to gain first team experience, where he suffered a compound facture of the leg and was out of action for a year. He was released by United after four seasons and signed for Macclesfield Town. Tomlinson now works as a DJ.

TRANTER, Wilf

Appearances: 1 Goals: 0 (1963-1966)
Career: *Manchester United, Brighton, Fulham (1963-1972)*. Signed for United as an apprentice straight from school in May 196, and became a professional 23 months later. He was only 19 when he made his only first team appearance in place of Billy Foulkes in March 1964, for a 2-0 win over West Ham, marking Johnny Byrne out of the game. After failing to break into the first team again, he was given a free transfer in May 1966 and moved to Brighton. Went into coaching with Swindon, then managed non-league sides Witney Town, Banbury United and Hungerford Town. Is now retired living in Faringdon, Oxfordshire.

TURNBULL, Jimmy

Appearances: 76 Goals: 42 (1907-1910)
Career: *Preston North End, Manchester United, Bradford Park Avenue, Chelsea (1905-1914)*. Formed a lethal partnership with his namesake Sandy, for the price of a friendly with Southern League Leyton. He collected a Championship title in his first season, a FA Cup winner's medal in his second season and then another league Championship before leaving, because he didn't have an agreement for a fourth season. He was to return to the club on a month's trial in 1914 but United's board refused to pay the £300 asking price with war imminent. He went into business in the Chorlton area of Manchester, where he ran a highly prosperous money lending business. He died in the city in 1945.

TURNBULL, Sandy

Appearances: 245 Goals:100 (1906-1915) Career: Manchester City, Manchester United (1902-1915). Controversy was never far away during his career. He was due to sign for Bolton until he received a better offer from City. He was then one of a number of players banned in an illegal payments scandal, becoming one of four to cross the great City divide. He became the first player sent off in a United-City derby in 1908, the year he contributed 25 goals to their title success. In 1909, he scored the winning goal in the FA Cup Final and before scoring 18 goals as United, won a second league title. His career ended under a cloud when he was banned for life for betting irregularities. He joined Footballers Battalion for the Great War and was killed in action in Arras, France, in May 1917.

TURNER, Chris

Appearances: 79 Goals: 0 (1985-1988) Career: Sheffield Wednesday, Lincoln City, Sunderland, Manchester United, Sheffield Wednesday, Leeds United, Leyton Orient (1976-1994). Joined in 1985 from Sunderland for £275,000 but had to wait until mid-season for his chance, and when Gary Bailey was forced to retire from the game through injury, he became first choice, only to lose his place to Gary Walsh. Sir Alex Ferguson then brought in Jim Leighton and it spelt the end of Turner's hopes of winning his place back, and he left for one of his previous clubs, Sheffield Wednesday in 1988, in a £175,000 deal. Three years later, he was a League Cup Final winner against United. Went into management with Leyton Orient where he was in joint charge with John Sitton. Has also been in charge at Wednesday and Stockport and is currently in the Hartlepool hot seat where he has the title of Director of Sport.

TWISS, Michael

Appearances: 2 Goals: 0 (1997-2000) Career: Manchester United, Sheffield United, Chester City, Morecombe (1997-2010). Born in Salford and joined United straight from school in 1994. A reserve team regular, he made his first team debut as a sub in a FA Cup tie with Barnsley. But he had only one other first team appearance in a league defeat against Aston Villa before being handed a free transfer by Morecombe in March 2010. Is now playing for Altrincham.

Photo: davidyoungphoto.co.uk

URE, Ian

Appearances: 64 Goals: 1 (1969-1971) Career: Arsenal, Manchester United (1963-1973). Blond-haired defender signed from Arsenal for £80,000 in 1969, and was the only major signing by Wilf McGuinness as cover for Bill Foulkes who was coming to the end of his brilliant career. He brought an upturn in fortunes but when Matt Busby regained control of the first team, he lost his place to Paul Edwards. And with his best days behind him, he was allowed to join St. Mirren on a free transfer. Returned to Glasgow in 1977 to work as a social worker in Barlinnie Prison in Glasgow before moving on to Low Moss Prison in Kilmarnock. Has now retired.

VAN DER GOUW, Raimond

Appearances: 60 Goals: 0 (1996-2002)
Career: *Manchester United, West Ham United (1985-2003).* Cost United £500,000 but it wasn't until 1999-2000 that he played enough games to claim a Premier League winner's medal, when he was often selected ahead of Mark Bosnich. The arrival of Fabien Barthez relegated him back to being second choice keeper but he still managed to become the oldest player to play for the club since World War two in May 2002. He spent six years at Old Trafford before leaving for West Ham, after turning down the chance of joining Coventry City. Upon retirement, Van der Gouw was signed as a goalkeeping coach for Sunderland before taking up a similar role at Vitesse Arnhem.

VAN NISTELROOY, Ruud

Appearances: 219 Goals: 150 (2001-2006) Career: *Manchester United (2001-2006).* A £19 million signing from PSV Edinhoven in April 2001, he will be remembered as one of the club's greatest ever goal scorers. But the deal almost didn't happen after he damaged knee ligaments in 2000, when he was on the verge of joining and the move was postponed. Despite having to pay £500,000 more for him, United signed

Photo: Nicholas MacGowan

him when he was fit. Sir Alex Ferguson acknowledges it was his son Darren who alerted him about Van Nistelrooy when he was on trial in Holland. A United legend, he sent the records tumbling during his five seasons at the club including scoring in the most number of consecutive matches, and for scoring the most goals in the Champions League. But he announced that he wanted to leave the club in July 2006 following reports of bust ups in training, and he moved to Real Madrid. In January 2010, he joined Hamburg on an 18 month contract.

Photo: Articularnos

VERON, Juan Sebastian

Appearances: 82 Goals: 11 (2001-2003)
Career: *Manchester United, Chelsea (2001-2007).* Moved from Lazio to Manchester United on 12 July 2001 for £28.1 million in a five year deal, the most expensive transfer in English football at the time. But he struggled to adapt to the pace of the English game and after only two seasons, he was sold to Chelsea for £15 million. Although he was widely seen as one of the most expensive flops in the club's history he was included in the FIFA 100 centenary list of the 125 greatest living footballers. Has been playing in Argentina for Estudianates since 2007 and was part of Argentina's 2010 World Cup squad.

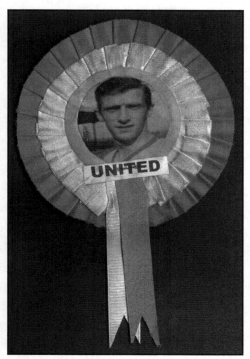

Photo: Leslie Millman

VIOLLET, Dennis

Appearances: 293 Goals: 179 (1952-1962) Career: Manchester United, Stoke City (1952-1966). A traditional centre forward whose two England caps are scant reward for his consistent goal scoring. In 1959-1960 alone he managed to find the net on 32 occasions in only 36 matches. He forged a profitable strike with Tommy Taylor until the Munich disaster took his partner's life. He was laid low for a long time after the crash but returned to action in time to play in the FA Cup Final against Bolton Wanderers. It came as a surprise when Sir Matt Busby sold him to Stoke City in 1962 for £25,000. In 1967, he moved to the United States as one of the pioneers of the sport in America. Was directing the Dennis Viollet Dolphin Soccer Camps in addition to his duties as head coach at Jacksonville University until his death in March 1999, after a battle with cancer. Daughter Rachel was the number one British women's tennis player.

WALDRON, Colin

Appearances: 4 Goals: 0 (1976-1978) Career: Bury, Chelsea, Burnley, Manchester United, Sunderland, Rochdale (1966-1979). Was signed by Tommy Docherty after nine seasons at Burnley, but was loaned to Sunderland after only playing four first team games. Ironically he had made his United debut at Roker Park in the League Cup in October 1976. He was released in April 1978 and moved to America to play for Tulsa Roughnecks. Now runs Waldron Racing in Nelson, and previously had business interests with Colin Bell in Bury.

WALKER, Dennis

Appearances: 1 Goals: 0 (1961-1963) Career: Manchester United, York City, Cambridge United (1961-1972). Wrote himself into the history books when he became United's first ever black player. He made his debut against Nottingham Forest in May 1963, just five days before the FA Cup Final against Leicester City but it proved to be his only first team appearance, and he joined York City. Had a spell as manager of Poole then a stint in South Africa, before returning to the UK where he worked as operations manager of the Arndale shopping complex. He was working there at the the time of a terrorist attack in 1996. Died in Stockport in August 2003, aged 58.

WALL, George

Appearances: 316 Goals: 98 (1906-1915) Career: Barnsley, Manchester United, Oldham Athletic, Rochdale (1903-1923). Signed for a bargain £175, he was one of the great outside lefts, pre-Great War. He scored the first of his 98 goals on his debut. Very fast and tricky, he was a key player in the two League successes and an FA Cup Final victory. He was sold to Oldham for £200 after the war, when he was a sergeant in the Black Watch. The England international worked on Manchester's Docks for many years after his retirement, and died in 1962, aged 77.

WALLACE, Danny

Appearances: 71 Goals: 11 (1989-1994)
Career: Southampton, Manchester
United, Millwall, Birmingham City,
Wycombe W (1980-1995). Never really
shone at United in the style that had led
to his £1 million move from Southampton
in 1989, when Sir Alex Ferguson needed
more experience on the left wing after
Lee Sharpe started the season as first
choice. He won a FA Cup winner's
medal against Crystal Palace. Sharpe
then regained his place in the side and
Wallace was a non-playing sub in the
Cup Winners Cup Final but he found
himself completely out of the first team
picture when Ryan Giggs burst onto the
scene. He left Old Trafford for £250,000
in October 1993 for Birmingham, after a
loan spell at Millwall. He was forced to
retire after being diagnosed with
multiple sclerosis, and has featured in an
advert for the MS Society. Has also set
up the Danny Wallace Foundation.

WALLWORK, Ronnie

Appearances: 28 Goals: 0 (1995-2002)
Career: Manchester United, Carlisle U,
Stockport C, WBA, Bradford C,
Barnsley, Huddersfield T Sheffield Wed
(1995-2008). A lifelong United fan who
was born in Newton Heath, he joined
the club as a trainee in April 1993,
turning professional two years later. He
helped United win the FA Youth Cup in
1995 and was named the club's Young
Player of the Year 12 months later. He
was a regular in the United reserve
team when he made his debut in
October 1997 in a 7-0 win over
Barnsley. He was banned for life for
grabbing a referee by the throat during
a spell at Royal Antwerp, but it was later
reduced on appeal. In 2000-2001, he
played enough games to qualify for a
Premier League winner's medal but
after the 2001-2002 season, his contract
wasn't renewed. Started a clothes
business, D&R Designers in Failsworth.

WALSH, Billy

Appearances:2 Goals: 0
Career: Manchester United war time
guest. (1942-1943). He played two
games against Liverpool at the end of
the 1942-1943 seasons. Ironically, he
was a junior at Old Trafford over a
decade previously but decided to join
Manchester City. He went into
management and succeeded Bill
Shankly at Grimsby, he later moved to
Australia where he worked for Norwich
Union in Melbourne while managing a
couple of local teams. He retired to
Noosa, Queensland, where he died in
July 2006 aged 85, three years after
attending the last match at Maine Road.
His Ashes are interned at the Garden of
Remembrance at the City of Manchester
Stadium.

WALSH, Gary

Appearances: 63 Goals: 0 (1986-1995)
Career: Manchester United, Oldham
Athletic, Middlesbrough, Bradford City,
Wigan Athletic (1985-2006). An
England Under-21 whose United career
was marred by injuries, he made his
debut as an 18 year old and later in
1986-1987 he had displaced Chris
Turner from the United first team. But
two head injuries saw Turner (who is
now his boss Hartlepool) back into the
team. He then fell behind Jim Leighton
in the pecking order. An ankle injury
kept him out of action for the best part
of two seasons and by the time he was
fit again, Peter Schmeichel was at the
club. He moved on to Middlesbrough in
1995. After retirement in 2006, Walsh
had already become player-
goalkeeping coach of his last club,
Wigan Athletic, and after officially
hanging up his boots, he continued his
coaching role with Derby County and
currently Hartlepool United. Has worked
with many of today's top keepers and
has also set up his own goalkeeping
academy.

WALTON, Joe

Appearances: 23 Goals: 0 (1945-1948)
Career: *Manchester United, Preston North End, Accrington Stanley (1940-1962).* A full back who had the misfortune to be at Old Trafford at the same time as Johnny Carey and John Aston, in the final season of war time football he was a regular in the United side. But in the first season after the war, he suffered a knee injury which kept him out of action for a couple of months and when he was fit again, he was unable to dislodge Carey from the side and was sold to Preston for £10,000, the highest fee ever paid for a full back. He stayed in Preston running a newsagents' before working for an electrical firm. Died in December 2006.

WALTON, John

Appearances: 3 Goals: 0 (1951-1952)
Career: *Bury, Manchester United, Bury, Burnley, Coventry City, Chester City (1949-1959).* An amateur during his time at Old Trafford which enabled him to win three England amateur caps when he was at the club. His only two league games for United came in 1951, when he stood in for Johnny Downie in successive matches. When he retired from the game, he lived in Chorley and was a teacher at Horwich Grammar School until his death in July 1979.

WARDLE, Alan

Career: *Manchester United (1960-1964).* A centre half in the juniors before moving to left back for the reserves, also played at right back. Left the club in April 1964. He opened his own office supplies company in Manchester.

WARNER, John

Appearances: 116 Goals: 2 (1938-1951)
Career: *Swansea Town, Manchester United, Oldham Athletic, Rochdale (1934-1953).* Capable of playing either in defence or attack, Warner had already been selected for Wales before his transfer from Swansea in 1938.

He managed one more international appearance before the war interrupted his career. Following the resumption of the league, he and Jack Pearson where the only survivors from the last game before the war. He lost his first team place before the 1948 FA Cup Final, and later became reserve team skipper. The Welshman stayed with United until 1951 when he moved the short distance to Oldham Athletic. He had a spell as player manager of Rochdale before opening a betting shop in Stretford, just two miles from Old Trafford. He retired to Tonypandy in Glamorgan and died in October 1980, aged 69.

WATSON, Willie

Appearances: 14 Goals: 0 (1970-1973)
Career: *Manchester United, Huddersfield Town (1970-1973).* A right back who took no prisoners, Watson was offered a professional contract on his 17th birthday but it wasn't until the short reign of Wilf McGuinness that he broke into the first team squad. He made his league debut against Blackpool at Old Trafford in September 1970, playing eight games before Matt Busby took over and dropped him. He had to wait until Tommy Docherty was manager before being called upon again, but was released at the end of that season and joined Miami Toros. Is now coaching in the USA with Banat Soccer Club, Arizona. Has also coached in Scottsdale.

WEALANDS, Jeff

Appearances: 8 Goals: 0 (1983-1985)
Career: *Wolves, Northampton, Darlington, Hull City, Birmingham, Manchester United, Oldham, Preston (1968-1985).* Joined United on loan as cover for Gary Bailey after he had fallen out with Birmingham City manager, Ron Saunders. He then signed permanent in August 1983 but a back injury restricted his appearances. Served on the board of Altrincham, worked in insurance, and coached the keepers at Bury for a while. Now works in property development.

WEBB, Neil

Appearances: 110 Goals: 11 (1989-1992) Career: Reading, Portsmouth, Nottingham Forest, Manchester United, Swindon Town, Grimsby Town, Aldershot (1980-1997). Signed for £1.5 million from Nottingham Forest at a time when Sir Alex Ferguson started to spend big in a bid to win silverware, and he started to repay his fee when he scored against Arsenal on his debut. Unfortunately, after just a handful of games for the club, he snapped his Achilles tendon playing for England and when he returned to action, he wasn't the same player. But he was still part of United's teams that won the FA Cup in 1990, Cup Winners Cup in 1991 and the League Cup a year later. He returned to the City Ground for only £800,000 in November 1992. Won 26 England caps and played for three more clubs before ending up at Weymouth.. Fell on hard times, was seen selling programmes outside the Madejski Stadium then worked as a postman. Is currently working hard for a transport company and as a part-time pundit. Son of Dougie who was a professional with Reading .

WEBBER, Danny

Appearances: 2 Goals: 0 (1999-2003) Career: Manchester United, Port Vale, Watford, Sheffield United, Portsmouth (1999-2010). He started out by signing as a trainee in July 1998 and signed a professional deal 18 months later after making an impact for the Under-17s. His progress continued into the Under-19s and reserves, eventually making his first team debut in a League Cup tie against Sunderland in November 2000. But following spells on loan, he was allowed to join Watford as part of the compensation package for Chris Eagles. He is now plying his trade at Portsmouth, joining as a free agent in September 2009.

WEBSTER, Colin

Appearances: 79 Goals: 31 (1953-1959) Career: Cardiff City, Manchester United, Swansea City, Newport County (1950-1964). Webster had won an Army Cup winner's medal before joining Manchester United in May 1952, after being recommended by his former Northern Command team mate, Dennis Viollet. Traditionally a centre forward, he was never a regular in the first team before Munich, a trip he missed out on because of a severe bout of the flu. After retiring, he worked as a scaffolder and for nine years as a park ranger in Swansea, where he died from lung cancer in March 2001, aged 68.

WELLENS, Richie

Appearances: 0 Goals: 0 (1999-2000) Career: Manchester United, Blackpool, Oldham Athletic, Doncaster Rovers, Leicester City (1999-2010). Played alongside the likes of Wes Brown during his two seasons in the youth team. Was given a pro contract in 1999 but left after a year to join Blackpool without playing a first team game. Signed for Leicester in a £1.2 million deal in July 2009.

WHALLEY, Arthur

Appearances: 106 Goals: 6 (1909-1920) Career: Blackpool, Manchester United, Southend United, Charlton Athletic, Millwall (1908-1926). Signed as a centre half for £50 from Blackpool after playing just five games. The following season, he won a League Championship medal after playing 15 games. But it wasn't for another three seasons until he became a regular, only then for a knee injury to check his progress. He resumed his career after the Great War but then left after one season, when he was sold to Southend for £1,000. He served in the Footballers Battalion during the Great War and was seriously wounded during the battle for Passchendale. When he retired, he became a bookmaker in Manchester. He died in Wythenshawe in 1952, aged 66.

Norman Whiteside mural. *Photo: G Travels*

WHALLEY, Bert

Appearances: 39 Goals: 0 (1935-1947)
Career: *Manchester United (1935-1947).* Whalley only played 39 games for United because of the Second World War. He was fast approaching the end of his career when normal league football resumed, and after just a handful of first team games an eye injury forced him to retire. The Methodist lay preacher joined the United coaching staff looking after the development of Busby Babes. He lost his life at Munich, aged just 45, after making the trip because Jimmy Murphy was managing Wales in Cardiff. His body was cremated at Dunkinfield Crematorium, Cheshire.

WHELAN, Liam

Appearances: 98 Goals: 52 (1954-1958)
Career: *Manchester United (1953-1958).* Spotted by Billy Behan playing for Home Farm and made his United debut in the FA Youth Cup Final against Wolves. He won two League medals, the First Division championship and the Central League. The following season United retained their crown with Whelan scoring 26 goals in 39 games. He shared the inside right birth with Bobby Charlton and missed the fateful clash with Red Star Belgrade only to perish on the way home at Munich. Is now buried in the Glasnevin Cemetery, Dublin.

WHELAN, Tony

Appearances: 0 Goals: 0 (1968-1973)
Career: *Manchester United, Manchester City, Rochdale (1969-1977).* Spotted by United scout, Joe Armstrong, and signed as an apprentice. Enjoyed a lot of success with the Youth team before signing a professional contract in 1969. He toured North America with the first team but never made it into a squad for a league or cup game, despite being leading scorer for the reserves in 1971-1972. Was about to sign for Bolton when City boss, Malcolm Allison, stepped in and he moved to Maine Road. Coached on Manchester City's Football in the Community programme until Brian Kidd invited him to coach at United's Academy, where he is now assistant Academy director.

WHITEFOOT, Jeff

Appearances: 95 Goals: 0 (1949-1956)
Career: *Manchester United, Grimsby Town, Nottingham Forest (1949-1967).* Jeff joined the United staff as an office boy. He became a regular when he took Don Gibson's place at right half and went on to became a member of the 1955-1956 championship winning squad. With his path to the first team blocked, he was allowed to leave the club and looked set to sign for Nottingham Forest until a last minute change of mind saw him go to Grimsby. He later moved to the City Ground. Whitefoot later became a licensee of the Wheatsheaf in Oakham, Rutland.

WHITEHURST, Walter

Appearances: 1 Goals: 0 (1952-1956)
Career: *Manchester United, Chesterfield, Crewe Alexandra, Chesterfield, Macclesfield Town (1952-1961).* Joined United in 1950 from the same Ryder Brow Boys Club that had supplied Roger Byrne only two years earlier. He signed a professional contract in 1952 but had to wait three years until the 1955-1956 Championship winning season to make his league debut. It turned out that the defeat at the hands of Everton in September 1955 was his only first team appearance. After being unable to dislodge Jeff Whitefoot and Eddie Colman in his six years at Old Trafford, he was sold to Chesterfield. Went into teaching and spent 27 years at Saint Aidan's Church of England Technology College until retiring. Now lives in retirement in Hambleton, Poulton le Flyde.

Photo: Sporting Memorabilia

WHITESIDE, Norman

Appearances: 274 Goals: 67 (1981-1989) Career: Manchester United, Everton (1981-1990). The history books will show how Norman became the youngest player to score at Wembley, and with Northern Ireland he broke the record for the youngest player to appear in the World Cup finals. He was also the first player to score in FA Cup and League Cup Finals in the same season. Norman notched up a total of over 250 appearances in a United shirt but under Sir Alex Ferguson, he struggled to find his form and was allowed to leave for Everton in a £750,000 deal in August 1989. Had it not been for persistent knee trouble which forced his retirement at the age of 25 in 1991, the same volumes may well have contained much, much more. Was a full-time student at Salford University where he studied Podiatry and works for the PFA, is a successful after dinner speaker, and also works as a match day host at Old Trafford.

WILKINS, Ray

Appearances: 194 Goals: 10 (1979-1984) Career: Chelsea, Manchester United, QPR Crystal Palace, QPR, Wycombe Wanderers, Hibernian, Millwall, Leyton Orient (1973-1997). Already a star through his exploits at Chelsea, 'Butch' quickly justified his £825,000 price tag following a 1979 move to Old Trafford. Still only 22 at the time of his signing, he developed into an admirable captain of both club and country. He was seen as being key to United's push to win the League Championship under Ron Atkinson. It was an unfortunate injury to his cheek bone that initially opened the door for Brian Robson to get his hands on both jobs. He scored a stunning goal in the FA Cup Final against Brighton but he was soon on his way to join AC Milan for £1.5 million. A glorious career began at Chelsea, with a debut in 1973 at the age of 17. Has managed QPR and Fulham, held various other coaching and management jobs and is currently assistant manager of Chelsea. He also provided the voice-over for Tango adverts in the 1990s.

Ray Wilkins
Photo: illarterate

WILKINSON, Ian

Appearances: 1 Goals: 0 (1991-1993)
Career: *Manchester United, Stockport County, Crewe Alexandra (1991-1995).*
A youth goalkeeping team mate of Ryan Giggs, cleaned the boots of Bryan Robson and Mark Hughes, made his only appearance for United in a League Cup tie second leg against Cambridge United. But after a couple of serious injuries, he was released and joined Stockport County. Had to quit the game because of a detached retina, qualified as a physio, still lives in Manchester and is a qualified doctor.

WILLIAMS, Ben

Appearances: 0 Goals: 0 (2002-2004)
Career: *Manchester United, Coventry City, Chesterfield, Crewe Alexandra, Carlisle United, Colchester United (2002-2010).* A Manchester born goalkeeper who started out as a trainee. He made the first team bench a couple of times when Fabian Barthez was injured but was released in 2004 without ever playing a first team game. went on to play for a number of clubs and most recently became a £60,000 signing for Colchester in July 2009.

WILLIAMS, Oshor

Appearances: 0 Goals: 0 (1976)
Career: *Manchester United, Southampton, Exeter City, Stockport County, Port Vale, Preston North End (1976-1987).* Was given a chance by United after he was released by Middlesbrough after three years as an apprentice, but he failed to make an impact at Old Trafford and was allowed to leave the club after only a season, without playing a first team game. Became a full-time student at Salford University studying history and politics, lectured in sports studies on a part-time basis at Trafford College, and now works for the PFA education service.

WILSON, David

Appearances: 6 Goals: 0 (1988-1991)
Career: *Manchester United, Lincoln City, Charlton A, Bristol R (1987-1993).* The centre midfielder worked his way through the ranks, juniors, reserves and into the first team squad. He made his debut as a sub in November 1988 for Clayton Blackmore in a game with Sheffield Wednesday. He went on to make five more appearances, all as a substitute, then after two spells on loan, was allowed to leave the club for Bristol Rovers. He moved to Sweden, where he has managed Ljungskile, and Sundsvall

WILSON, Mark

Appearances: 10 Goals: 0 (1997-2001)
Career: *Manchester United, Wrexham, Middlesbrough, Stoke , Swansea City, Doncaster R, Tranmere R (1997-2010).* He started out as a trainee in August 1997. He made his debut a season later and appeared in the Premier League and Champions League before he was sold to Middlesbrough, along with Jonathan Greening, in a £1.5 million in August 2001. He joined Doncaster Rovers in November 2007, following a spell in the States with FC Dallas.

WINTERBOTTOM, Walter

Appearances: 27 Goals: 0 (1936-1938)
Career: *Manchester United (1936-1938).* A school teacher before being spotted by Louis Rocca, he was named as one of the twelve discoveries of the 1937-1938 season by Topical Times. Made his debut against Leeds United standing in for George Vose, and went on to keep Vose out of the side when he returned to fitness. He looked a centre half of genuine promise but a back injury ended his career. A wing commander during the Second World War, he was appointed the FA's director of coaching and managed England between 1947-1962. Became secretary of the Central Council of Physical Recreation. He died in February 2002, aged 89.

WOOD, Neil

Appearances: 0 Goals: 0 (1999-2006)
Career: *Manchester United,*
Peterborough United, Burnley, Coventry
City, Blackpool, Oldham Athletic (1999-
2007). A Manchester born midfielder,
he was a regular member of the reserve
team squad where he was rated highly
enough to be appointed captain. He
had five spells out on loan but never
broke into the United first team squad.
He later played in Bosnia but has
dropped into non-league football with
Athertone Town. He is based in
Tamworth and works as a postman, as
well as playing for Bolehall Swifts in the
Midlands Combination Premier.

WOOD, Nicky

Appearances: 4 Goals: 0 (1983-1989)
Career: *Manchester United (1983-1989).*
An England youth international, he
combined playing with studying
Economics at Manchester University.
He made his league debut as a sub
against Everton on Boxing Day 1985. He
started his first game under the reign of
Sir Alex Ferguson against Nottingham
Forest in March 1987, but was troubled
by back problems and after specialist's
advice in January 1989, he was forced to
quit the game. Is believed to living in
the Greater Manchester area.

WOOD, Ray

Appearances: 208 Goals: 0 (1949-1959)
Career: *Darlington, Manchester United,*
Huddersfield Town, Bradford City,
Barnsley (1949-1967). Ray had only
played a dozen games for Darlington
when United paid £5,500 to take him to
Old Trafford, and he went straight into
the first team to play against Newcastle
United, the club who had shown him the
door only six months earlier. He to
battle Reg Allen and Jack Crompton for
a place in the first team so ended up
playing the odd 'A' team game as centre
forward and working in a textile
warehouse. When he finally established
himself, he won two League winner's
medals and was the victim of an horrific
Peter McParland challenge in the 1957
Cup Final. He later survived Munich
only to lose his place to Harry Gregg
and was sold to Huddersfield Town for
£1,500 in December 1958. He qualified
as a FA coach and held many coaching
jobs around the world. Settled in Bexhill,
Sussex, he ran a sportswear company
and then took charge of a suit department
in a Hastings department store until his
retirement. He died in July 2002, aged 71.

WOODS, Gary

Appearances: 0 Goals: 0 (2008)
Career: *Manchester United, Doncaster*
Rovers (2008-2010). Signed by United
from Cambridge United in July 2007,
after he had trials at a number of Premier
League clubs including Arsenal. But he
was released in the summer of 2008
after being hampered by injuries. Signed
for Doncaster Rovers in March 2009.

WORTHINGTON, Frank

Worthington, who is one of the great
football mavericks was part of the
United squad which toured Australia
after the 1983-1984 season making
appearances against Australia,
Nottingham Forest and Juventus. He
played another game for the club in
May 1985 in Peter Foley's testimonial
against Oxford United. After a spell as
player manager of Tranmere Rovers, he
has become an in demand after dinner
speaker.

Photo: Antonia Sterland

WRATTEN, Paul

*Appearances: 2 Goals: 0 (1990-1992)
Career: Manchester United, Hartlepool
United, York City (1990-1994).* Born in
Middlesbrough, he joined United from
school in the summer of 1987. He made
two appearances against Wimbledon
and Crystal Palace as a substitute. He
suffered two stress fractures of the legs
which cost him 18 months and led to his
release at the end of the 1991-1992
season. He is now living in Dingleby
Barwick near Stockton-on-Tees.

WRIGGLESWORTH, Billy

*Appearances: 37 Goals: 10 (1936-1947)
Career: Chesterfield, Wolves,
Manchester United, Bolton Wanderers,
Southampton, Reading (1932-1949).* A
coal miner before becoming a
professional footballer. He scored on
his home debut against Preston but lost
a large chunk of his career at the club
due to the Second World War. He left
United for Bolton just after league
football resumed after the war. His
playing career ended and he coached
at a school in the South, before
returning north to become the trainer of
Accrington Stanley. He continued to live
a stone's throw away from Peel Park until
his death in August 1980, aged 67.

Dwight Yorke
Photo: caribbeanfreephoto

YORKE, Dwight

*Appearances: 152 Goals: 66 (1998-
2002) Career: Aston Villa, Manchester
United, Blackburn R, Birmingham C,
Sydney FC, Sunderland (1989-2009).*
The 'Smiling Assassin' joined United for
£12.6 million in August 1998 and was a
key player in his first season, forming a
formidable partnership with Andy Cole.
He ended the season as leading scorer
with 18 goals. He lost his way after
tensions with Sir Alex over his relationship
with glamour model Jordan. He was
eventually sold to Blackburn Rovers at
the end of that season for £2 million.
Yorke was briefly made player assistant
manager at Sunderland during the
2008-2009 season following Roy Keane's
departure. He is currently the sports
ambassador for Trinidad and Tobago,
and in 2009 released his autobiography
called "Born To Score". Has recently
appeared as a pundit on Sky Sports.

YOUNG, Tony

*Appearances: 79 Goals: 1 (1971-1976)
Career: Manchester United, Charlton
Athletic, York City (1969-1978).* He
became a regular in Tommy Docherty's
struggling side of 1972-1973. He
started in midfield before moving to
right back where he took the place of
Tommy O'Neill. He lost his place
midway through the relegation season
when Stewart Houston was signed. He
only played 15 games when United
returned to the First Division, enough to
win a medal but he was later released
on a free transfer and spent eight
months at Charlton. Lives in Runcorn
and has worked at Manchester Airport.

ZIELER, Ron-Robert

*Appearances: 0 Goals: 0 (2008-2010)
Career: Manchester United, Northampton
(2008-2010).* Joined United as a trainee
in July 2005 and won Manchester and
Lancashire Senior Cup winner's medals
before he was released in the summer
of 2010. He signed for Hannover 96
following a successful trial in April 2010.

MANAGERS & MORE

Ernest Mangnall

His legacy should be remembered alongside Sir Matt Busby and Sir Alex Ferguson, he turned United into a force with the help of brewery owner John Henry Davies. Within three seasons of taking over at the club they were promoted. Then after bringing in the likes of Billy Meredith and Sandy Turnbull, he turned them into a Championship winning side. He left United for City in 1912, staying for 12 years. He later became a director of Bolton Wanderers and died in Lytham St Annes in January 1932 aged 66.

John Robson

Officially United's first ever titled manager and remained in charge for seven years, the longest reign under Sir Matt Busby took his record. World War One took away four years of stay at the club and when he quit through ill heath in October 1921 he helped his successor John Chapman until his death just a year later.

John Chapman

After only winning of his first 15 games in charge it was no surprise that United where relegated at the end of Chapman's first season in charge. The rebuilding job took three years but he finally got them promoted in 1925. He looked to have them moving in the right direction again when a letter from the Football Association arrived at Old Trafford suspending him after alleging misconduct. But the charges were never made public and United were left with little option other than to sack him. He became the manager of a greyhound stadium and later a director of Plymouth Argyle before his death in December 1948 aged 66.

Clarence Hilditch

See players section

Herbert Bamlett

A top referee before going into management he took charge of the 1914 FA Cup Final. He arrived at Old Trafford with extensive management experience gained at Oldham Athletic, Wigan Borough and Middlesbrough. But he found a club in decline and at the end of the 1930-31 when United finished bottom of the table and were relegated they parted company. He never worked in management again and died in October 1941.

Walter Crickmer

One of the finest administrators in United history, even though he was secretary he had a spell in charge of team selection between the reigns of Bamlett and A Scott Duncan. Then when Duncan left before World War Two and the appointed of Sir Matt Busby throughout the troubled times of the war years. He started work at United in 1926 and stayed until his death in the Munich Air Crash after 38 years service. He is buried in Stretford Cemetery.

A Scott Duncan

In June 1932 was appointed United manager on a salary of £800 a year after making one appearance for the club as a guest during the World War One. Despite spending heavily on players United were almost relegated to the Third Division in 1933-34. But he managed to turn things around and in 1935-36 and led the club to promotion. But he resigned a year later to manage Southern League Ipswich Town. Then remained at Portman Road as manager until 1955 after a couple of years as general manager he retired to Helensburgh, Scotland where he lived until his death in October 1975 aged 87.

Sir Matt Busby

Appointing Matt Busby is widely seen as the most significant decision taken by United. He was wanted by Liverpool as a coach, Reading as assistant manager and Ayr United as manager. But they landed their man after offering him £15 a week. They then hung onto him after Spurs offered him £50 a week to move to London in 1949. He was given the last rites following Munich because of the seriousness of his injuries, but returned to work after six months. Twice in his time in charge of the club he built great teams, the first being whipped out by the Munich Air Crash. The second went onto become the first English team to win the European Cup in 1968, which earned him a knighthood. By the time he retired in 1971 after a second short spell in charge of United, they had won five league titles, five Charity Shield's, the FA Cup twice and the European Cup. He became general manager and then was appointed a director of United and was mentioned in the Beatles song Dig It. He died in Manchester from cancer aged 84 in January 1994 and is buried in Southern Cemetery, Manchester.

Jimmy Murphy

Was appointed Matt Busby's right hand man after his boss heard him give a speech to troops. He was put in charge of scouting and nurturing the Busby Babes. He missed Munich because he was managing Wales at the time but took charge of rebuilding while Busby was critically ill in hospital. He stayed by Busby's side until 1971, when he retired but continued to scout for the club. He died in November 1989 aged 79. United's Young Player of the Year award is named after him.

Wilf McGuinness

See players section

Frank O'Farrell

Lured away from Leicester City in June 1971 but he could replicate the same success he enjoyed at Filbert Street. United blew a five point lead in his first season in charge and it was all downhill from there. He tried and failed to halt the slide with the chairman's chequebook and was sacked in December 1972. Went onto manage Cardiff, Torquay, Iran and in the UAE he now quietly lives in retirement in the Devon resort.

Tommy Docherty

The Doc was one of the most colourful characters in management when he succeeded Frank O'Farrell with just enough time to steer the club away from relegation. But it only proved to be a temporary reprieve despite spending money they were relegated the following season. Life in the second tier only lasted a season as they swept to the Second Division title. He appeared to be building a side that could challenge again after two FA Cup Final appearances in as many years only to be sacked after an affair with the wife of physio Laurie Brown was made public. He went onto manage in England and abroad but never with the same success, he is still in demand as an after dinner speaker.

Dave Sexton

Sexton was the fourth manager in eight seasons at Old Trafford but was seen as someone who could bring some stability. He was given plenty of financial backing to bring the league title back to the club. Despite reaching a third FA Cup Final in four seasons, improving the league position took time. The club record signing of Ray Wilkins helped them finish second to Liverpool but after slipping back into mid-table obscurity he was sacked. Sexton twice managed the England under-21 team either side of managing Coventry, he was the first Technical Director at the FA's National School at Lilleshall in 1984, and he now lives in retirement in Kenilworth, Warks.

Photo: Antonia Sterland

Ron Atkinson

If it was possible to be the complete opposite of your predecessor then United found it in Atkinson. Bundles of charisma and sparkle but it wasn't enough to end the clubs wait to land a league title. And despite spells of heavy spending which included Bryan Robson and Frank Stapleton he only had two FA Cup's and two Charity Shields to show for his five years at Old Trafford. It looked as if they were finally going to deliver in 1985-86 after winning ten games on the trot they were clear at the top of the table. But injuries robbed them of several key stars they slumped. Atkinson was eventually replaced by Sir Alex Ferguson. He stayed in management before embarking on a media career which almost came to an abrupt end following a storm over racist remarks.

Mick Brown

Ron Atkinson's assistant returned to United after spells at Bolton and abroad, also Coventry where he was chief scout. He had to retire from Old Trafford when he reached 65. Has since worked for WBA and Sunderland and is now scouting for Spurs.

Louis Rocca

Worked for Newton Heath and then United for half a century mainly as the clubs fixer in chief. He claimed that changing the name to United was his brainchild. He discovered a number of top stars and put the club in touch with Matt Busby in 1945, five years before his death.

Tommy Cavanagh

The Doc's right hand man left United in 1981, had spells with Newcastle, Tronheim and Burnley. His last job was at the FA's Centre of Excellence at Lilleshall until he retired. He was diagnosed with Alzheimer's in March 2002. He died in March 2007 aged 78.

Tom Curry

A trainer who was bought to Old Trafford by A Scott Duncan and then stayed on when Sir Matt Busby joined the club after World War Two. And he still held the position when he travelled to Yugoslavia with the first team squad for an ill fated trip which saw him lose his life in the Munich Air Crash. He was cremated at Manchester Crematorium.

Joe Armstrong

Succeeded Louis Rocca as chief scout and discovered many of the Busby Babes including Duncan Edwards as well as Bobby Charlton. He died in 1975.

Louis Rocca
Photo: Leslie Millman

Acknowledgements

Many thanks must go to, Tony Park, David Sadler of Manchester United Former Players Association, Arthur Albiston, Andrew Kilduff at Stretford End Flags, Mick Green, Mark Harrop, James Motley at Sky TV., Brigitte Baker, Katharine Pringle, United Nights.

Bibliography

The PFA Premier League and Football League Record 1949-1998.
Hugman, Barry J

An English Football Internationals Who's who Lamming, D.

The Breedon Book of Football Managers.
Turner, Dennis & White Alex.

Where Are They Now.
Pringle Andy, Fissler, Neil.

Manchester United A Complete Record 1878-1990.
Morrison Ian, Slury Alan.

Manchester United player by player.
Ponting Ivan.

The United Alphabet – A Complete Who's Who of Manchester United
Dykes, Gareth.

Where Are They Now Chelsea FC.
Fissler Neil, Andy Pringle.

Websites

Two fantastic websites have made this task so much easier and we are grateful to everyone who contributes to...

Wikipedia: www.wikipedia.com
Flikr: www.flikr.com

Photographs

A:3KFootball flickr.com/photos/a3k1
Ajburgess flickr.com/photos/ajburgess
AlBakker flickr.com/photos/aibakker
Andy Welsh flickr.com/photos/wallrevolution
Andybrannan flickr.com/photos/andybrannan
Antonio Jordana flickr.com/photos/aj
Articularnos flickr.com/photos/articularnos
Austin Knight flickr.com/photos/austinknight
Babasu flickr.com/photos/babasu
Bashvaldo e298.photobucket.com/home/bashvaldo
Beatriz Martinez flickr.com/photos/7322590@N07
Bernt Rostad flickr.com/photos/brostad
Brett Robertson flickr.com/photos/7991011@N08
Brizzlechris flickr.com/photos/brizzlechris
Caribbeanfreephoto flickr.com/photos/georgiap
CamW en.wikipedia.org/wiki/User:Camw
chas2112 flickr.com/photos/27517898@N07
chelsea_steve flickr.com/photos/27449997@N06
Dan Mullen flickr.com/photos/dan_mullen
David Mullen flickr.com/photos/scousemoj
Dullhunk flickr.com/photos/dullhunk
edwin.11 flickr.com/photos/edwin11
egghead06 en.wikipedia.org/wiki/User:Egghead06
Fee (df82) flickr.com/photos/21743020@N07
Fendyzaiden flickr.com/photos/beckzaidan
Global Imagination flickr.com/photos/magicplanet
Globovisión flickr.com/photos/globovision
Gordon Flood gordonflood.com
Gustavo Bravo flickr.com/photos/aguapixelada
Illarterate flickr.com/photos/illarterate
Jackashgone flickr.com/photos/andrew_ashton
Las Orejas de Ringo flickr.com/photos/pampanitos
Mcshanebest flickr.com/photos/mcshanebest
Meygun flickr.com/photos/meimeiengineer
N.VTM flickr.com/photos/48594829@N03
Ned Trifle www.flickr.com/photos/nedtrifle
Nicholas MacGowan flickr.com/photos/nmacca
Nicksarebi flickr.com/photos/34517490@N00
Nigel Wilson flickr.com/photos/cocca
O. Taillon Photography flickr.com/photos/olitaillon
Omar_Gurnah flickr.com/photos/omargurnah
Paul-Ipswich flickr.com/photos/11017253@N06
Ray Haslam flickr.com/photos/54596905@N00
Ronnie Macdonald flickr.com/photos/ronmacphotos
ruth1066 flickr.com/photos/ruth1066
Stephen Broadhurst flickr.com/photos/31845030@N08
Steve Montgomery flickr.com/photos/scuba04
terry 6082 Books flickr.com/photos/terry6082books
The Labour Party www.flickr.com/photos/labourparty
Toksuede flickr.com/photos/ryusha
Tuborg Light en.wikipedia.org/wiki/User:TuborgLight
UJMi flickr.com/photos/ujmi/
US Marine Corps flickr.com/photos/marine_corps
Visitmanchester flickr.com/photos/visitmanchester
Ypauleau flickr.com/photos/ypauleau
and a special thank you to
Leslie Millman
flickr.com/photos/manchesterunitedman1